slow cookers

Published in 2008 by Murdoch Books Pty Limited.
www.murdochbooks.com.au

Murdoch Books Australia
Pier 8/9, 23 Hickson Road
Millers Point NSW 2000
Phone: + 61 (O) 2 8220 2000
Fax: + 61 (O) 2 8220 2558

Murdoch Books UK Limited
Erico House, 6th Floor
93-99 Upper Richmond Road
Putney, London SW15 2TG
Phone: + 44 (O) 20 8785 5995
Fax: + 44 (O) 20 8785 5985

Chief Executive: Juliet Rogers
Publishing Director: Kay Scarlett

Design Manager: Vivien Valk
Concept: Sarah Odgers
Art Direction & Design: Heather Menzies
Editor: Kim Rowney
Food Editor: Alison Adams
Production: Kita George
Photographer: Jared Fowler
Stylist: Cherise Koch
Food preparation: Alan Wilson
Introduction text: Leanne Kitchen
Recipes developed by Alison Adams, Peta Dent, Michelle Earl, Vicky Harris
and the Murdoch Books Test Kitchen

National Library of Australia Cataloguing-in-Publication entry
Author: Price, Jane (Jane Paula Wynn)
Title: Slow cookers / Jane Price.
ISBN: 978 1 74196 226 0 (pbk.)
Series: Kitchen classics
Notes: Includes index.
Subjects: Electric cookery, Slow
Dewey Number: 5884

A catalogue record for this book is available from the British Library

Colour reproduction by Splitting Image Colour Studio, Melbourne, Australia.
Printed by 1010 Printing International Ltd. in 2008. PRINTED IN CHINA.
Reprinted 2008.

IMPORTANT: Those who might be at risk from the effects of salmonella poisoning (the elderly, pregnant women, young children and those suffering from
immune deficiency diseases) should consult their doctor with any concerns about eating raw eggs.
CONVERSION GUIDE: You may find cooking times vary depending on the oven you are using. For fan-forced ovens, as a general rule, set the oven temperature
to 20°C (35°F) lower than indicated in the recipe.

The publisher would like to thank Sunbeam Corporation Limited for providing the slow cookers used in this book.

slow cookers

THE SLOW COOKER RECIPES
YOU MUST HAVE

SERIES EDITOR **JANE PRICE**

MURDOCH BOOKS

CONTENTS

HEARTY FAMILY FARE

Trends come and go, and when it comes to kitchen gadgetry, we've possibly seen them all. From omelette makers, ice-cream machines and bread makers to plug-in tagines and electric tin openers, it seems there's been an electrical appliance invented for every culinary situation imaginable. Yet how many of us have succumbed to the latest, greatest gizmo, only to discover that it takes up too much space in our cupboards or is annoyingly hard to clean? Having said that, there are some machines and appliances we'd rather not live without. Food processors, blenders and electric beaters have removed a great deal of tedious elbow grease from much of our cooking and we'd be hard pressed to cook successfully without them. Slow cookers are another indispensable kitchen device that no busy household should be without. They've been around since the 1960s and have always had their devotees, but more and more cooks are wising up to the time- and budget-saving capabilities of the slow cooker.

Slow cookers transform many foods (particularly those tougher, tastier cuts of meat) from their raw state to melting tenderness, with not much more exertion than flicking a switch. They can be plugged in anywhere, they use less electricity than your oven, and there is only one bowl to wash up afterwards. You don't need to stir or hover over a meal simmering in a slow cooker and it's almost impossible to burn anything; there's such latitude in cooking times that an hour or two more isn't going to make much difference. In a slow cooker, meals practically cook themselves and they taste incredible — every last drop of the food's natural flavour is captured inside the cooker.

From hearty soups such as seafood chowder and pea and ham soup to creamy chicken curry, country beef stew and lamb shanks in red wine, the hardest thing about using your slow cooker will be deciding what to make in it.

Slow cookers are also called 'Crock Pots'; Crock Pot is a brand name that was conjured up in America in 1971. Essentially, a slow cooker is an electrical appliance, comprising a round, oval or oblong cooking vessel made of glazed ceramic or porcelain. This is surrounded by a metal housing, which contains a thermostatically controlled element. The lid, which is often transparent, makes it easy to check the progress of what's cooking inside. The recipes in this book were developed using a 4.5 litre (157 fl oz/18 cup) slow cooker but they come in a variety of sizes, with the largest having a capacity of around 7 litres (245 fl oz/28 cups). Note that slow cookers work best when they are at least half, and preferably three-quarters, full (the operating manual that comes with your model will advise you on this).

Most models of slow cookers have a number of temperature settings and typically these are 'low', 'medium' and 'high'. The 'low' setting cooks foods at around 80°C (175°F) while 'high' cooks foods at around 90°C (195°F). 'Medium' is a combination of these two temperatures; when set to medium the slow cooker cooks for around an hour at 'high', then automatically clicks to 'low' and continues cooking at that temperature. As a general rule, cooking on 'low' doubles the cooking time from a 'high' setting and you can tweak the cooking times of recipes to longer or shorter. Recipe cooking times vary from 3 to 12 hours.

At its simplest, to use your slow cooker all you need to do is prepare and chop your ingredients, add liquid (water, wine or stock) and turn it on, leaving the contents to murmur away until cooked to lush tenderness. Time-strapped cooks can put ingredients in the slow cooker before work and return home at night to a dinner ready-to-go; or, meals can be cooked overnight. The cooking environment in a slow cooker is very moist, making it perfect for tough cuts of meat such as beef blade, lamb or veal shanks, or pork belly. Such cuts contain a great quantity of connective tissues and these can only be broken down with long, slow cooking. When preparing meat, it is important that you trim fatty meat well, as the fat tends to settle on top of the juices.

The slow cooker requires less liquid than normal stovetop or oven cookery, as there is no chance for the liquid to evaporate. In fact, many foods, including some meats, release moisture of their own during cooking (up to one cup per average recipe), so bear this in mind when you think a recipe doesn't have enough liquid in it, or when adapting recipes for the slow cooker (when adapting standard recipes for the slow cooker cut the liquid by 50 per cent). Resist the urge to lift the lid during cooking, particularly at the beginning, as the slow cooker takes a while to heat up, and always cook with the lid on unless the recipe instructs otherwise — perhaps when thickening a sauce. If you need to remove the lid to stir or to check the food is cooked, replace the lid quickly so the slow cooker doesn't lose too much heat.

It is difficult to overcook tougher meats but it is possible (the meat will turn raggedy and fall apart into thin shreds) so you still need to use the suggested cooking times for each recipe. Keep in mind, however, that cooking times may vary, depending on the brand and size of slow cooker you are using. And, because cooking times are fairly approximate, we have rounded our cooking times to the nearest 15 minutes.

While most recipes use the slow cooker as a true one-pot solution, where everything goes in together at the start, other recipes use the cooker as the primary mode of cooking but use other steps along the way. Optionally you can brown meats such as pork, beef or lamb on the stovetop first, before adding them to the cooker. Meat gains extra flavour when browned, as the outside surfaces caramelise over high temperatures (about 100°C/210°F) and this cannot be achieved in a slow cooker. Recipes in the entertaining chapter of this book include this extra step but for any meat recipe, you can choose to brown first if you like.

Hard vegetables such as root vegetables can take a very long time to cook, so cut them into smallish pieces and push them to the base of the cooker or around the side, where the heat is slightly greater. Green vegetables can lose some nutrients if cooked for prolonged periods, so blanch them first (if required) and add them at the end of cooking to heat through. Seafood and dairy products should also be added to the slow cooker near the end of cooking.

FOOD SAFETY

In the past there have been concerns about food safety issues with slow cookers, namely whether harmful bacteria that are present in foods, particularly in meats, are killed at such low temperatures. However, bacteria are killed off at around 68°C (155°F), so users of slow cookers need not be concerned about bacteria. One rule here though is to never place meats that are still frozen, or partially frozen, in a slow cooker as this scenario can cause food-poisoning bacteria to flourish; ALWAYS have meats thawed fully before cooking. And never use the ceramic insert after it has been frozen or refrigerated as the sudden change in temperature could cause it to crack.

Another caveat is that you cannot cook dried red kidney beans from their raw state in the slow cooker because the temperature is not high enough to destroy the natural toxins found in these beans. Dried red kidney beans, and other dried beans, need to be boiled for 10 minutes to destroy these toxins. Tinned beans however are safe for immediate use. To prepare dried beans, soak the beans in water for 5 hours or overnight. Discard the water, then rapidly boil the beans in fresh water for 10 minutes to destroy the toxins.

* Make sure you read the manufacturer's instructions for the safe use of your slow cooker.

SOUPS

FRENCH ONION SOUP

20 g (³/₄ oz) butter
1 tablespoon olive oil
1 kg (2 lb 4 oz) brown onions, thinly sliced
250 ml (9 fl oz/1 cup) dry white wine
2 tablespoons brandy (optional)
750 ml (26 fl oz/3 cups) beef stock
4 thyme sprigs
2 tablespoons finely chopped flat-leaf (Italian) parsley

SERVES 4

Put the butter, olive oil and onion in the slow cooker. Cook on low for 4 hours, stirring occasionally.

Add the wine, brandy (if using), stock, 250 ml (9 fl oz/1 cup) water and thyme. Cook on high for a further 2 hours. Season to taste with salt and freshly ground black pepper. Sprinkle with the parsley and serve with crusty bread.

PREPARATION TIME: 20 MINUTES   COOKING TIME: 6 HOURS

POTATO AND LEEK SOUP

4 all-purpose potatoes, roughly chopped
2 leeks, white part only, thinly sliced
2 celery stalks, chopped
1 carrot, chopped
2 prosciutto slices, roughly chopped
500 ml (17 fl oz/2 cups) chicken or vegetable stock
pouring cream, to serve

SERVES 4

Put the potato, leek, celery, carrot, prosciutto, stock and 500 ml (17 fl oz/ 2 cups) water in the slow cooker. Cook on high for 3 hours.

Using a hand-held stick blender, purée the soup until smooth. Alternatively, transfer the soup mixture to a food processor and purée until smooth. Season to taste with salt and freshly ground black pepper. Ladle the soup into bowls and serve drizzled with cream.

PREPARATION TIME: 10 MINUTES   COOKING TIME: 3 HOURS

French onion soup

CREAM OF MUSHROOM SOUP

10 g (¹/₄ oz) dried porcini mushrooms
1 leek, white part only, thinly sliced
100 g (3¹/₂ oz) pancetta or bacon,
chopped
200 g (7 oz) Swiss brown mushrooms,
roughly chopped
300 g (10¹/₂ oz) large field mushrooms,
roughly chopped
125 ml (4 fl oz/¹/₂ cup) Madeira (Malmsey)
(see Note)
1 litre (35 fl oz/4 cups) chicken or
vegetable stock
2 teaspoons chopped marjoram
90 g (3¹/₄ oz/¹/₃ cup) light sour cream or
crème fraîche
marjoram leaves, extra, to garnish

SERVES 4

Soak the porcini in 250 ml (9 fl oz/1 cup) boiling water for 20 minutes. Drain, reserving the soaking water.

Combine the porcini and the soaking water, leek, pancetta or bacon, Swiss brown and field mushrooms, Madeira, stock and half of the chopped marjoram in the slow cooker. Cook on high for 2 hours.

Using a hand-held stick blender, purée the soup. Alternatively, transfer the soup mixture to a food processor and purée until smooth, then return the soup to the slow cooker.

Stir through the sour cream and cook for a further 5 minutes, then stir through the remaining chopped marjoram. Garnish with marjoram leaves and serve with crusty bread.

PREPARATION TIME: 20 MINUTES +   COOKING TIME: 2 HOURS

NOTE: Madeira is a fortified wine made in Portugal. Malmsey is the richest and fruitiest of the Madeiras and it can also be drunk as an after-dinner drink. If unavailable, use sherry.

VEGETABLE AND CHEDDAR SOUP

2 all-purpose potatoes (about 250 g/9 oz), diced
2 zucchini (courgettes), diced
1 carrot, diced
1 celery stalk, diced
3 spring onions (scallions), finely chopped
1 litre (35 fl oz/4 cups) chicken or vegetable stock
425 g (15 oz) tinned creamed corn
125 g (4^1/$_2$ oz/1 cup) grated cheddar cheese
2 tablespoons finely chopped flat-leaf (Italian) parsley

SERVES 4

Put the potato, zucchini, carrot, celery and spring onion in the slow cooker. Add the stock and season well with salt and freshly ground black pepper. Cook on high for 3–4 hours, or until the vegetables are cooked.

Just before serving, stir in the creamed corn, cheese and parsley. Season to taste with salt and pepper. Serve when the cheese has just melted and the soup has heated through.

PREPARATION TIME: 15 MINUTES   COOKING TIME: 3–4 HOURS

NOTE: If preferred, you can add some barbecued shredded chicken or chopped ham at the end of cooking, at the same time as the corn and cheddar cheese.

CAULIFLOWER AND ALMOND SOUP

1 large leek, white part only, chopped
2 garlic cloves, crushed
1 kg (2 lb 4 oz) cauliflower, cut into small florets
2 all-purpose potatoes, such as desiree, (about 370 g/13 oz), diced
1.5 litres (52 fl oz/6 cups) chicken stock
75 g (2^1/$_2$ oz/^{1}/$_2$ cup) blanched almonds, chopped
20 g (^{3}/$_4$ oz/^{1}/$_3$ cup) snipped chives
pouring cream, to serve

SERVES 4

Put the leek, garlic, cauliflower, potato and stock in the slow cooker. Cook on high for 3 hours, or until the potato and cauliflower are tender.

Using a hand-held stick blender, purée the soup with the almonds. Alternatively, transfer to a food processor and purée until smooth. Stir through half the chives and season with salt and freshly ground black pepper. Ladle the soup into bowls, drizzle with cream and garnish with the remaining chives.

PREPARATION TIME: 20 MINUTES   COOKING TIME: 3 HOURS

NOTE: The soup will thicken on standing. Stir through extra stock if desired.

Vegetable and cheddar soup

CALDO VERDE

6 all-purpose potatoes, chopped
1 red onion, chopped
2 garlic cloves, crushed
750 ml (26 fl oz/3 cups) vegetable stock
60 ml (2 fl oz/¼ cup) olive oil
1 chorizo sausage (about 180 g/6½ oz), diced
500 g (1 lb 2 oz) silverbeet (Swiss chard) or kale, thinly sliced

SERVES 4

Put the potato, onion, garlic, stock and olive oil in the slow cooker. Cook on high for 3 hours, or until the potato is cooked.

Using a hand-held stick blender, purée until smooth. Alternatively, transfer to a food processor and blend until smooth. Return to the slow cooker along with the chorizo and silverbeet and cook for a further 1 hour on low. Season to taste with salt and freshly ground black pepper.

PREPARATION TIME: 15 MINUTES   COOKING TIME: 4 HOURS

BUTTERNUT PUMPKIN SOUP

1.25 kg (2 lb 12 oz) butternut pumpkin (squash), peeled, seeded and chopped into even-sized chunks
1 all-purpose potato, chopped
1 onion, chopped
1 carrot, chopped
2 teaspoons ground cumin
1 teaspoon freshly grated nutmeg
750 ml (26 fl oz/3 cups) chicken or vegetable stock
60 ml (2 fl oz/¼ cup) pouring cream
1 tablespoon chopped flat-leaf (Italian) parsley, to garnish

SERVES 4

Put the pumpkin, potato, onion and carrot in the slow cooker. Sprinkle over the cumin and nutmeg and season with salt and freshly ground black pepper. Stir to coat the vegetables in the spices. Pour over the stock. Cook on high for 3 hours, or until the pumpkin is tender.

Using a hand-held stick blender, purée until smooth. Alternatively, transfer to a food processor and purée until smooth. Drizzle with cream and scatter over the parsley before serving.

PREPARATION TIME: 15 MINUTES   COOKING TIME: 3 HOURS

RIBOLLITA

800 g (1 lb 12 oz) tinned cannellini beans, drained and rinsed
400 g (14 oz) tinned chopped tomatoes
1 garlic clove, crushed
1 carrot, diced
1 celery stalk, thinly sliced diagonally
1/4 cabbage, thinly shredded
300 g (10 1/2 oz) all-purpose potatoes, cut into 1 cm (1/2 inch) dice
2 tablespoons tomato paste (concentrated purée)
2 tablespoons extra virgin olive oil
1 litre (35 fl oz/4 cups) chicken stock
200 g (7 oz) 'pane de casa' or crusty bread, broken into small chunks
50 g (1 3/4 oz/1/2 cup) freshly grated parmesan cheese

SERVES 6

Place half the cannellini beans and the tomatoes in the bowl of a food processor. Process until puréed.

Put the bean and tomato purée in the slow cooker along with the garlic, carrot, celery, cabbage, potato, tomato paste, olive oil and stock. Stir to combine. Cook on high for 4 hours, or until the vegetables are cooked.

Taste and check for seasoning. Add the remaining cannellini beans, bread chunks and parmesan. Stir and cook for a further 5 minutes, or until the cheese has melted, then serve.

PREPARATION TIME: 20 MINUTES   COOKING TIME: 4 HOURS

NOTE: Ribollita literally means 'reboiled' and is a traditional Tuscan soup, often made in large quantities and reheated again the next day.

PEA AND HAM SOUP

2 onions, finely chopped
2 carrots, finely chopped
2 celery stalks, finely chopped
1 turnip, finely chopped
440 g (15^1/$_2$ oz/2 cups) split green peas, rinsed and drained
1 smoked ham hock (800 g/1 lb 12 oz) (see Note)
1 litre (35 fl oz/4 cups) chicken stock
2 bay leaves
2 thyme sprigs

SERVES 6–8

Put the onion, carrot, celery, turnip, peas, ham hock, stock, 1 litre (35 fl oz/ 4 cups) water, bay leaves and thyme in the slow cooker. Cook on low for 8 hours, or until the peas are very soft and the ham is falling off the bone.

Remove the ham bones and meat. When cool enough to handle, cut off any meat still attached to the bone, then cut the meat into small pieces. Return the meat to the soup. Season to taste with salt and freshly ground black pepper.

PREPARATION TIME: 15 MINUTES   COOKING TIME: 8 HOURS

NOTE: Ask your butcher to cut the ham hock into smaller pieces for you.

TOMATO, SPINACH AND RISONI SOUP

1 leek, white part only, thinly sliced
1 garlic clove, crushed
^{1}/$_2$ teaspoon ground cumin
500 g (1 lb 2 oz/2 cups) tomato passata (puréed tomatoes)
750 ml (26 fl oz/3 cups) chicken or vegetable stock
200 g (7 oz/1 cup) risoni (see Note)
200 g (7 oz) smoked ham, chopped (optional)
500 g (1 lb 2 oz) English spinach, trimmed, leaves sliced
1^1/$_2$ tablespoons lemon juice

SERVES 4

Put the leek, garlic, cumin, passata, stock and 500 ml (17 fl oz/2 cups) water in the slow cooker. Cook on low for 3 hours.

Place the risoni in a heatproof bowl and cover with boiling water. Set aside for 10 minutes, then drain. Add to the slow cooker along with the ham (if using). Cook for a further 30 minutes, or until the risoni is tender.

Stir through the spinach and lemon juice and cook, stirring, until the spinach is wilted. Season to taste with salt and freshly ground black pepper. Serve with crusty bread.

PREPARATION TIME: 15 MINUTES   COOKING TIME: 3^1/$_2$ HOURS

NOTE: Risoni looks like rice but is actually a type of pasta, often used in soups and stews. If unavailable, use any type of small soup pasta.

PASTA AND BEAN SOUP

1 onion, finely chopped
1 small celery stalk, finely chopped
1 carrot, finely chopped
1 smoked ham hock, about 500 g
(1 lb 2 oz), skin scored
400 g (14 oz) tinned chopped tomatoes
750 ml (26 fl oz/3 cups) chicken stock
1 bay leaf
1 large rosemary sprig
400 g (14 oz) tinned red kidney beans,
drained and rinsed
150 g (5¹/₂ oz/1 cup) macaroni pasta
2 tablespoons chopped flat-leaf
(Italian) parsley

SERVES 6

Combine the onion, celery, carrot, ham hock, tomatoes, stock, 1.5 litres (52 fl oz/6 cups) water, bay leaf and rosemary in the slow cooker. Cook on low for 6 hours. Remove the ham hock and allow to cool slightly.

Add the beans and macaroni to the slow cooker. Increase the heat to high and cook for a further 30 minutes, or until the pasta is *al dente*.

When cool enough to handle, remove the meat from the ham hock, discarding the fat and bone. Cut the meat into small pieces and return to the slow cooker. Stir through the parsley and season to taste with salt and freshly ground black pepper. Serve immediately.

PREPARATION TIME: 30 MINUTES   COOKING TIME: 6¹/₂ HOURS

NOTE: This Italian pasta and bean (*pasta e fagioli*) soup is very thick. If preferred, stir in a little more stock at the end of cooking to thin it.

MINESTRONE

1 onion, finely chopped
2 garlic cloves, crushed
80 g (2³/₄ oz) pancetta or bacon, diced
1 carrot, diced
2 all-purpose potatoes, cut into
1 cm (¹/₂ inch) dice
1 celery stalk, halved lengthways, sliced
700 g (1 lb 9 oz) tomato passata
(puréed tomatoes)
750 ml (26 fl oz/3 cups) chicken or
vegetable stock
100 g (3¹/₂ oz) ditalini or macaroni pasta
100 g (3¹/₂ oz) green beans, cut into
2 cm (³/₄ inch) pieces
100 g (3¹/₂ oz) English spinach leaves,
shredded
400 g (14 oz) tinned cannellini beans,
drained and rinsed
1 small handful basil, torn
1 small handful flat-leaf (Italian) parsley,
roughly chopped
freshly grated parmesan cheese, to serve

SERVES 6–8

Put the onion, garlic, pancetta, carrot, potato, celery, tomato passata, stock and 750 ml (26 fl oz/3 cups) water in the slow cooker. Cook on low for 8 hours.

Put the pasta in a heatproof bowl, cover with boiling water and soak for 10 minutes. Drain.

Add the drained pasta, green beans, spinach and cannellini beans to the slow cooker. Cook, uncovered, for a further 30 minutes, or until the pasta is *al dente* and the vegetables are tender.

Stir through the basil and parsley and season to taste with salt and freshly ground black pepper. Ladle the soup into bowls and sprinkle with the parmesan. Serve with crusty bread.

PREPARATION TIME: 30 MINUTES   COOKING TIME: 8¹/₂ HOURS

RAVIOLI SOUP

1 small leek, white part only
3 silverbeet (Swiss chard) leaves
1 carrot, diced
1 zucchini (courgette), diced
1 celery stalk, including some leaves, diced
2 whole dried Chinese mushrooms
1.5 litres (52 fl oz/6 cups) chicken stock
1 tablespoon light soy sauce
250 g (9 oz) fresh ravioli pasta, such as chicken and mushroom

SERVES 4

Leave the root attached to the leek and slice lengthways a few times. Wash thoroughly under cold water to remove any grit, then drain. Chop into small pieces, discarding the root.

Wash the silverbeet leaves and cut away the thick white stems. Tear the leaves into smaller pieces. Set aside.

Put the leek, carrot, zucchini and celery in the slow cooker. Add the Chinese mushrooms, then pour in the stock and soy sauce. Cook on high for 3-4 hours, or until the vegetables are cooked. About 30 minutes before the end of cooking time, add the silverbeet and ravioli. Cover and continue to cook for a further 20 minutes until the pasta is *al dente*.

Using kitchen tongs, remove the mushrooms, discard the stems, then thinly slice the mushroom caps and return them to the soup. To serve, ladle the soup and pasta into serving bowls and sprinkle with freshly ground black pepper.

PREPARATION TIME: 20 MINUTES   COOKING TIME: 3-4 HOURS

NOTE: For a vegetarian version, use vegetable stock and a vegetable filled ravioli.

SEAFOOD CHOWDER

500 g (1 lb 2 oz) skinless firm white
fish fillets (see Note)
100 g (3¹/2 oz) smoked ham, diced
3 large all-purpose potatoes, cut into
1 cm (¹/2 inch) dice
2 leeks, white part only, thinly sliced
3 large garlic cloves, crushed
1.125 litres (39 fl oz/4¹/2 cups) fish or
chicken stock
1 bay leaf
3 thyme sprigs
20 scallops (about 350 g/12 oz),
without roe
290 g (10¹/4 oz) tinned baby clams,
undrained
430 ml (15 fl oz/1³/4 cups) thickened
(whipping) cream
2 tablespoons chopped flat-leaf
(Italian) parsley

SERVES 4–6

Cut the fish fillets into 2 cm (³/4 inch) cubes, then cover and refrigerate
until needed.

Put the ham, potato, leek, garlic, stock, bay leaf and thyme in the slow
cooker. Cook on high for 3 hours, or until the potato is tender.

Add the fish, scallops, clams and the liquor, and the cream. Cook for a
further 30 minutes, or until the fish is cooked. Season to taste with salt
and freshly ground black pepper. Stir in the parsley and serve with bread.

PREPARATION TIME: 30 MINUTES   COOKING TIME: 3¹/2 HOURS

NOTE: You can use any white fish fillets, such as swordfish or gemfish.

BOUILLABAISSE

2 tomatoes
1 carrot, chopped
1 celery stalk, chopped
1 leek, white part only, chopped
1 fennel bulb, roughly chopped
250 ml (9 fl oz/1 cup) fish stock
100 ml (3½ fl oz) white wine or pernod
2 garlic cloves, crushed
grated zest of 1 orange
pinch saffron threads
1 tablespoon tomato paste
(concentrated purée)
200 g (7 oz) firm white fish fillets,
such as monkfish
200 g (7 oz) salmon fillet
12 mussels
12 raw prawns (shrimp)
chopped flat-leaf (Italian) parsley, to serve

SERVES 6

Score a cross in the base of each tomato. Put the tomatoes in a heatproof bowl and cover with boiling water. Leave for 30 seconds, then transfer to cold water, drain and peel the skin away from the cross. Cut the tomatoes in half and roughly chop the flesh.

Put the tomatoes in the slow cooker along with the carrot, celery, leek, fennel, stock, wine, garlic, orange zest, saffron and tomato paste. Cook on high for 3 hours.

Meanwhile, prepare the seafood. Cut the white fish into 2 cm (³/₄ inch) pieces. Remove any bones from the salmon using your fingers or a pair of tweezers, and cut into 2 cm (³/₄ inch) pieces. Scrub the mussels with a stiff brush and pull out the hairy beards. Discard any broken mussels or open ones that don't close when tapped on the work surface. Peel the prawns, leaving the tails intact, then gently pull out the dark vein from each prawn back, starting at the head end. Refrigerate the seafood until needed.

After 3 hours cooking time, allow the soup base to cool slightly, then transfer the mixture to a food processor and blend until smooth. Return to the slow cooker along with the white fish and salmon and cook for a further 2 hours on low.

Add the mussels and prawns to the slow cooker and cook for a further 1 hour on low. Ladle the soup into large serving bowls and garnish with parsley. Serve with crusty bread.

PREPARATION TIME: 30 MINUTES   COOKING TIME: 6 HOURS

PRAWN GUMBO

1 onion, finely chopped
1 garlic clove, crushed
1 red capsicum (pepper), seeded and
chopped
4 bacon slices, trimmed of fat, diced
1^1/$_2$ teaspoons dried thyme
2 teaspoons dried oregano
1 teaspoon sweet paprika
^{1}/$_4$ teaspoon cayenne pepper
60 ml (2 fl oz/^{1}/$_4$ cup) dry sherry
1 litre (35 fl oz/4 cups) fish or light
chicken stock
100 g (3^1/$_2$ oz/^{1}/$_2$ cup) par-cooked
long-grain rice
2 bay leaves
400 g (14 oz) tinned chopped tomatoes
150 g (5^1/$_2$ oz) okra, sliced
1 kg (2 lb 4 oz) raw prawns (shrimp)

SERVES 4–6

Put the onion, garlic, capsicum, bacon, thyme, oregano, paprika, cayenne pepper, sherry, stock, rice, bay leaves, tomatoes and okra in the slow cooker. Cook on low for 4 hours, or until the rice is cooked and the okra is tender.

Meanwhile, prepare the prawns. Peel the prawns, leaving the tails intact, then gently pull out the dark vein from each prawn back, starting at the head end. Refrigerate until needed.

Stir in the prawns and cook for a further 15–20 minutes, or until the prawns are cooked through. Serve immediately.

PREPARATION TIME: 30 MINUTES   COOKING TIME: 4^1/$_4$ HOURS

THAI CHICKEN AND GALANGAL SOUP

2 x 5 cm (³/₄ x 2 inch) piece galangal, thinly sliced
500 ml (17 fl oz/2 cups) coconut milk
250 ml (9 fl oz/1 cup) chicken stock
4 makrut (kaffir lime) leaves, torn
1 tablespoon finely chopped coriander (cilantro) root, well rinsed
1–2 teaspoons finely chopped red chilli
500 g (1 lb 2 oz) boneless, skinless chicken breasts
2 tablespoons fish sauce
1¹/₂ tablespoons lime juice
3 teaspoons grated palm sugar (jaggery) or soft brown sugar
coriander (cilantro) leaves, to garnish

SERVES 4

Put the galangal, coconut milk, stock, half the lime leaves, coriander root and chilli in the slow cooker. Simmer on low for 1³/₄ hours.

Meanwhile, prepare the chicken. Trim off any fat and then cut the chicken into thin strips. Add the chicken strips, fish sauce, lime juice and palm sugar to the slow cooker and cook for a further 5–10 minutes, or until the chicken is cooked through. Stir through the remaining lime leaves.

Ladle the soup into serving bowls and garnish with the coriander leaves.

PREPARATION TIME: 20 MINUTES   COOKING TIME: 2 HOURS

TOM YUM

3 lemon grass stems, white part only
5–7 bird's eye chillies
3 thin slices galangal
2 litres (70 fl oz/8 cups) chicken stock or water
5 makrut (kaffir lime) leaves, torn
350 g (12 oz) raw prawns (shrimp)
90 g (3¹/₄ oz/¹/₂ cup) drained tinned straw mushrooms, or quartered button mushrooms
2 tablespoons fish sauce
60 ml (2 fl oz/¹/₄ cup) lime juice
2 teaspoons caster (superfine) sugar
coriander (cilantro) leaves, to garnish

SERVES 4

Use the handle of a knife or a rolling pin to bruise the white part of the lemon grass stems. Remove the stems from the chillies and bruise them with the knife handle or rolling pin.

Place the lemon grass, chillies, galangal, stock and 3 of the lime leaves in the slow cooker. Cook on high for 2 hours.

Meanwhile, prepare the prawns. Peel the prawns, leaving the tails intact. Gently pull out the dark vein from each prawn back, starting at the head end. Add the prawns and mushrooms to the slow cooker and cook for 5 minutes, or until the prawns are firm and pink. Stir through the fish sauce, lime juice and sugar. Taste, then adjust the seasoning with extra lime juice or fish sauce if necessary. Garnish the soup with coriander leaves before serving.

PREPARATION TIME: 30 MINUTES   COOKING TIME: 2 HOURS

CHICKEN LAKSA

CHICKEN BALLS
500 g (1 lb 2 oz) minced (ground) chicken
1 small red chilli, finely chopped
2 garlic cloves, finely chopped
1/2 small red onion, finely chopped
1 lemon grass stem, white part only,
finely chopped
2 tablespoons chopped coriander
(cilantro) leaves

70 g (2^1/2 oz/^{1}/4 cup) laksa paste
750 ml (26 fl oz/3 cups) chicken stock
500 ml (17 fl oz/2 cups) coconut milk
200 g (7 oz) dried rice vermicelli noodles
8 fried tofu puffs, halved diagonally
90 g (3^1/4 oz/1 cup) bean sprouts
2 tablespoons shredded Vietnamese mint
3 tablespoons coriander (cilantro) leaves
lime wedges, to serve

SERVES 4

To make the chicken balls, put the chicken, chilli, garlic, onion, lemon grass and chopped coriander in a food processor and process until just combined. Roll tablespoons of the mixture into balls with wet hands.

Put the chicken balls, laksa paste, stock and coconut milk in the slow cooker. Cook on high for 2^1/2 hours.

Put the vermicelli in a heatproof bowl, cover with boiling water and soak for 10 minutes. Drain well.

Divide the vermicelli, tofu puffs and bean sprouts among four serving bowls and ladle the soup over the top, dividing the chicken balls evenly. Garnish with the mint and coriander and serve with the lime wedges.

PREPARATION TIME: 30 MINUTES   COOKING TIME: 2^1/2 HOURS

MULLIGATAWNY SOUP

375 g (13 oz) boneless, skinless chicken thighs
2 tablespoons tomato chutney
1 tablespoon mild Indian curry paste
2 teaspoons lemon juice
$1/2$ teaspoon ground turmeric
1.25 litres (44 fl oz/5 cups) chicken stock
1 onion, finely chopped
1 all-purpose potato, diced
1 carrot, diced
1 celery stalk, diced
65 g ($2^1/4$ oz/$^1/3$ cup) basmati rice
2 tablespoons chopped coriander (cilantro) leaves

SERVES 4

Prepare the chicken by trimming off any fat, then cutting into small cubes.

Put the tomato chutney, curry paste, lemon juice and turmeric in the slow cooker and mix with some of the stock. Add the remaining stock. Add the chicken, onion, potato, carrot, celery and rice. Cook on high for 3–4 hours, or until the chicken, vegetables and rice are cooked.

Season to taste with salt and freshly ground black pepper. Ladle the soup into bowls and serve garnished with the coriander.

PREPARATION TIME: 30 MINUTES   COOKING TIME: 3–4 HOURS

NOTE: Add a little more Indian curry paste if you prefer a stronger curry flavour.

CANJA

3 tomatoes
200 g (7 oz/1 cup) long-grain rice
2.5 litres (87 fl oz/10 cups) chicken stock
1 onion, cut into thin wedges
1 celery stalk, finely chopped
1 teaspoon grated lemon zest
1 mint sprig
2 boneless, skinless chicken breasts
2 tablespoons lemon juice
2 tablespoons shredded mint

SERVES 6

Score a cross in the base of each tomato. Put the tomatoes in a heatproof bowl and cover with boiling water. Leave for 30 seconds, then transfer to cold water, drain and peel the skin away from the cross. Cut the tomatoes in half, scoop out the seeds and chop the flesh.

Combine the chopped tomatoes, rice, stock, onion, celery, lemon zest and mint in the slow cooker. Cook on high for 3 hours, or until the rice is tender.

Prepare the chicken by trimming off any fat, then cutting into thin slices. Add the chicken to the slow cooker, then add the lemon juice and stir for about 10 minutes, or until the chicken is cooked through. Season to taste with salt and freshly ground black pepper. Stir in the shredded mint just before serving.

PREPARATION TIME: 20 MINUTES   COOKING TIME: $3^1/4$ HOURS

CREAMY CHICKEN AND CORN SOUP

4 corn cobs
500 g (1 lb 2 oz) boneless, skinless chicken thighs, trimmed
2 garlic cloves, chopped
1 leek, white part only, chopped
1 large celery stalk, chopped
1 bay leaf
1/2 teaspoon thyme
1 litre (35 fl oz/4 cups) chicken stock
60 ml (2 fl oz/1/4 cup) sherry
1 large floury potato, such as russet, cut into 1 cm (1/2 inch) dice
185 ml (6 fl oz/3/4 cup) pouring cream
snipped chives, to garnish

SERVES 4–6

Using a large knife, remove the corn kernels from the cobs. Put the corn, chicken, garlic, leek, celery, bay leaf, thyme, stock, sherry and potato in the slow cooker. Cook on high for 2 hours.

Using kitchen tongs, remove the chicken to a board and allow to cool. Discard the bay leaf.

Purée the soup using a hand-held stick blender. When the chicken is cool enough to handle, shred the chicken and return the meat to the slow cooker, then pour in the cream. Cook for a further 10–15 minutes, or until the chicken is heated through. Garnish with chives before serving.

PREPARATION TIME: 20 MINUTES   COOKING TIME: 2¼ HOURS

CHICKEN SOUP

1.6 kg (3 lb 8 oz) chicken
1 leek, white part only, sliced
2 celery stalks, sliced
1 large carrot, chopped
1 parsnip, chopped
1 tablespoon chopped dill

SERVES 6

Put the chicken, leek, celery, carrot and parsnip in the slow cooker. Cover the chicken and vegetables with 2.5 litres (87 fl oz/10 cups) water. Cook on low for 8 hours, or until the chicken meat is falling off the bones.

Remove the chicken and, when cool enough to handle, remove the meat from the bones. Return the chicken meat to the slow cooker and cook for 5 minutes, or until heated through. Sprinkle with dill to serve.

PREPARATION TIME: 20 MINUTES   COOKING TIME: 8 HOURS

NOTE: If desired, transfer to a container and refrigerate overnight, then skim the fat from the top the next day.

June 2013
Super easy.
After soup is cooked, lift out chicken + let cool a bit before removing bones + skin. Place chicken in a tupperware. Refrigerate broth overnight + skim fat in the morning. Add 2 chopped potatoes to broth. Simmer until potatoes are cooked, then add chicken to soup.
If you have a container of Bryson Farm's curried squash soup, mix it in c̄ the chicken soup. Delicious! (Season loves the mixture)

Dec 2010

Cousin to Tom ha khai soup.
I'd add a splash of lime juice next time

CURRIED CHICKEN NOODLE SOUP

next time ↑ to 2-3 chillis

1 small red chilli, seeded and finely chopped

1 tablespoon finely chopped fresh ginger *↑ to 2 tbsp*

2 tablespoons Indian curry powder

750 ml (26 fl oz/3 cups) good-quality chicken stock

cans 800 ml (28 fl oz) tinned coconut milk

120 g (4¼ oz) dried rice vermicelli noodles

300 g (10½ oz) baby bok choy (pak choy)

lots (it shrinks right down) 2 x 250 g (9 oz) boneless, skinless chicken breasts

4 tablespoons torn basil *I whole bag from thai grocery store*

added 1 tsp salt

SERVES 6

Put the chilli, ginger, curry powder, stock and coconut milk in the slow cooker. Cook on high for 1½ hours.

Meanwhile, prepare the remaining ingredients. Put the vermicelli in a heatproof bowl, cover with boiling water and soak for 10 minutes, or until soft, then drain. Separate the bok choy leaves and slice the large leaves in half lengthways. Prepare the chicken by trimming off any fat, then cut it into thin slices.

Stir the vermicelli, bok choy and chicken through the soup. Cook for a further 20 minutes, or until the chicken is tender and cooked. Stir through the basil just before serving.

PREPARATION TIME: 25 MINUTES   COOKING TIME: 2 HOURS

made Dec 1/10 on a cold, very rainy day. Yummy! Don't forget to add 3 cups H₂O!

PORK CONGEE

used extra ginger. sprinkled c toasted sesame seeds in the bowls as well as sesame oil.

300 g (10½ oz/1½ cups) long-grain rice, rinsed thoroughly

↑ 2 1 star anise

2 spring onions (scallions), white part only, sliced

5 cm (2 inch) piece fresh ginger, thinly sliced

2 litres (70 fl oz/8 cups) chicken stock *Plus 3 cups water!*

↑ 2 1 garlic clove, crushed

400 g (14 oz) minced (ground) pork *used gr. chicken*

60 ml (2 fl oz/¼ cup) light soy sauce

white pepper, to season

sesame oil, to serve

fried bread sticks, to serve (optional)

SERVES 4

Put the rinsed rice, star anise, spring onion, ginger slices, stock, 750 ml (26 fl oz/3 cups) water, garlic and pork in the slow cooker. Cook on low for 5 hours, or until the rice has broken down and is a soupy consistency. Stir through the soy sauce and season with white pepper.

Taste and adjust the seasoning with extra white pepper if necessary. Drizzle with sesame oil and serve with fried bread sticks if desired.

PREPARATION TIME: 15 MINUTES   COOKING TIME: 5 HOURS

NOTES: Fried bread sticks are sold in Chinese stores. They are best eaten fresh on the day they are made.

The soup will thicken on standing. Add more water or chicken stock if desired.

BORSCHT BEEF

1.2 kg (2 lb 10 oz) chuck steak
1 onion, cut into 2 cm (3/4 inch) dice
2 celery stalks, cut into 2 cm
(3/4 inch) dice
2 beetroot (beets), peeled and cut
into wedges
1/2 small cabbage, cut into 2 cm
(3/4 inch) dice
3 tablespoons tomato paste
(concentrated purée)
400 g (14 oz) tinned chopped tomatoes
375 ml (13 fl oz/1 1/2 cups) beef stock
2 tablespoons vinegar
125 g (4 1/2 oz/1/2 cup) sour cream
2 tablespoons horseradish
squeeze of lemon juice
2 tablespoons chopped flat-leaf
(Italian) parsley

SERVES 4–6

Trim the beef of any fat and cut it into 2 cm (3/4 inch) cubes. Combine the beef, onion, celery, beetroot, cabbage, tomato paste, tomatoes, stock and vinegar in the slow cooker. Cook on high for 3 hours.

Remove the lid and continue to cook on high for a further 1 1/2–2 hours, or until the borscht reaches a thick casserole consistency. Season to taste with salt and freshly ground black pepper.

Combine the sour cream, horseradish and lemon juice in a bowl and season with salt. Serve the soup garnished with the horseradish cream and chopped parsley.

PREPARATION TIME: 20 MINUTES   COOKING TIME: 4 1/2–5 HOURS

BEEF PHO

500 g (1 lb 2 oz) piece gravy beef
5 cm (2 inch) piece fresh ginger,
thinly sliced
1.5 litres (52 fl oz/6 cups) beef stock
6 black peppercorns
1 cinnamon stick
4 cloves
6 coriander seeds
500 g (1 lb 2 oz) fresh thick rice noodles
2 tablespoons fish sauce
150 g (5¹/₂ oz) rump steak, very
thinly sliced
3 spring onions (scallions), finely
chopped
1 onion, very thinly sliced
3 tablespoons coriander (cilantro) leaves
chilli sauce or hoisin sauce, to serve

GARNISHES
red chillies, sliced
bean sprouts
purple basil leaves
spring onions (scallions), sliced diagonally
thin lime wedges

SERVES 6

Put the piece of gravy beef, ginger, stock, 250 ml (9 fl oz/1 cup) water, peppercorns, cinnamon stick, cloves, coriander seeds and 1 teaspoon salt in the slow cooker. Cook on low for 6 hours.

Using kitchen tongs, remove the beef and set aside to cool. Use a slotted spoon to remove the spices. When the beef is cool enough to touch, cut it across the grain into very thin slices. Set aside.

Add the rice noodles and fish sauce to the stock in the slow cooker. Cover and cook for 5 minutes, or until the noodles have softened.

Divide the noodles among the serving bowls. Place some slices of the cooked beef and a few slices of the raw steak on top of the noodles in each bowl. Ladle the hot stock over the top and sprinkle with the spring onion, onion slices and coriander leaves.

Arrange the garnishes on a platter in the centre of the table for each person to choose from. Serve with chilli or hoisin sauce to add to the soup, if desired.

PREPARATION TIME: 20 MINUTES   COOKING TIME: 6 HOURS

GOULASH SOUP WITH DUMPLINGS

1 kg (2 lb 4 oz) chuck steak
1 onion, finely chopped
1 garlic clove, crushed
2 tablespoons sweet paprika
pinch cayenne pepper
1 teaspoon caraway seeds
400 g (14 oz) tinned chopped tomatoes
750 ml (26 fl oz/3 cups) chicken stock
350 g (12 oz) all-purpose potatoes, cut
into 2 cm (³/4 inch) dice
1 green capsicum (pepper), halved,
seeded and cut into thin strips
2 tablespoons sour cream

DUMPLINGS
80 g (2³/4 oz/²/3 cup) self-raising flour
25 g (1 oz/¹/4 cup) finely grated parmesan
cheese
2 teaspoons finely chopped thyme
1 egg, lightly beaten

SERVES 6

Trim the steak of any fat and cut into 1 cm (¹/2 inch) cubes. Put the steak, onion, garlic, paprika, cayenne pepper, caraway seeds, tomatoes, stock and potato in the slow cooker. Cook on low for 4¹/2 hours, or until the beef is tender and the potato is cooked through.

Stir in the capsicum, then turn the slow cooker to high and cook for a further 1 hour with the lid off. Season to taste with salt and freshly ground black pepper.

To make the dumplings, put the flour and parmesan in a bowl. Season with salt and stir in the thyme and egg. Transfer the mixture to a floured surface and lightly knead to a soft dough. Using 1 teaspoon of the mixture at a time, roll it into a ball. Drop the dumplings into the slow cooker. Cover and cook on high for 10–15 minutes, or until the dumplings are cooked through.

Gently lift the dumplings out of the slow cooker and divide among serving bowls. Stir the sour cream into the soup and ladle the soup over the dumplings.

PREPARATION TIME: 30 MINUTES   COOKING TIME: 5³/4 HOURS

SUKIYAKI SOUP

1 teaspoon dashi granules
1 leek, white part only
10 g (1/4 oz) dried shiitake mushrooms, sliced
1.5 litres (52 fl oz/6 cups) chicken stock
125 ml (4 fl oz/1/2 cup) soy sauce
2 tablespoons mirin
1 1/2 tablespoons sugar
100 g (3 1/2 oz) Chinese cabbage, shredded
300 g (10 1/2 oz) silken firm tofu, cut into 2 cm (3/4 inch) cubes
400 g (14 oz) rump steak, thinly sliced
100 g (3 1/2 oz) dried rice vermicelli noodles
4 spring onions (scallions), sliced diagonally

SERVES 4–6

Put the dashi in a heatproof bowl with 500 ml (17 fl oz/2 cups) boiling water and stir until the granules have dissolved.

Leave the root attached to the leek and slice in half lengthways. Wash thoroughly under cold water to remove any grit, then drain. Thinly slice the leek, discarding the root.

Put the dashi, leek, mushrooms, stock, soy sauce, mirin and sugar in the slow cooker. Cook on low for 2 hours.

Add the Chinese cabbage and cook for a further 5 minutes, or until wilted. Stir through the tofu and beef and cook for a further 2 minutes, or until the beef is cooked through.

Meanwhile, place the vermicelli in a heatproof bowl, cover with boiling water and soak for 10 minutes, or until soft, then drain. Divide the noodles among the serving bowls and ladle on the soup. Serve garnished with the spring onion.

PREPARATION TIME: 30 MINUTES   COOKING TIME: 2 1/4 HOURS

HOME COOKING

SPIRALI WITH HAM, LEMON AND PEAS

500 g (1 lb 2 oz) spirali pasta
750 ml (26 fl oz/3 cups) chicken stock
250 ml (9 fl oz/1 cup) pouring cream
3 small thyme sprigs
1 large strip lemon zest
150 g (5^1/$_2$ oz) smoked ham, diced
2 eggs, lightly beaten
100 g (3^1/$_2$ oz/1 cup) freshly grated parmesan cheese
230 g (8 oz/1^1/$_2$ cups) fresh or frozen peas

SERVES 6

Put the spirali in a large heatproof bowl. Pour over boiling water and set aside, stirring occasionally, for 10 minutes.

Drain the pasta and place it in the slow cooker along with the stock, 625 ml (21 fl oz/2^1/$_2$ cups) water, cream, thyme and strip of lemon zest. Cook on low for 3 hours, or until the liquid has almost absorbed and the pasta is tender.

Stir in the ham, eggs, parmesan and peas. Cook, stirring occasionally, for 5–10 minutes, or until the peas are cooked and the sauce has thickened. Season to taste with salt and freshly ground black pepper before serving.

PREPARATION TIME: 20 MINUTES   COOKING TIME: 3^1/4 HOURS

ZUCCHINI AND RICOTTA CANNELLONI

2 zucchini (courgettes), grated
500 g (1 lb 2 oz) fresh ricotta cheese
2 teaspoons chopped rosemary
200 g (7 oz) dried cannelloni (about 20 tubes)
700 g (1 lb 9 oz) ready-made tomato pasta sauce
225 g (8 oz/1^1/$_2$ cups) grated mozzarella cheese
1 handful basil, chopped

SERVES 4–6

Combine the zucchini, ricotta and rosemary in a bowl. Season with salt and freshly ground black pepper. Use a teaspoon to fill the cannelloni tubes with the zucchini and ricotta mixture.

Place half of the filled cannelloni in the base of the slow cooker. Pour over half of the tomato pasta sauce to cover and then sprinkle with half the cheese and half the basil. Top with another layer of filled cannelloni and the remaining pasta sauce, cheese and basil.

Cook on high for 3 hours, or until the pasta is *al dente* and the cheese has melted. Serve with a green salad if desired.

PREPARATION TIME: 20 MINUTES   COOKING TIME: 3 HOURS

Spirali with ham, lemon and peas

MACARONI CHEESE

200 g (7 oz/2 cups) macaroni pasta
cooking oil spray
375 ml (13 oz) tinned evaporated milk
375 ml (13 fl oz/1¹/2 cups) full cream milk
3 eggs, lightly beaten
¹/2 teaspoon freshly grated nutmeg
3 spring onions (scallions), chopped
125 g (4¹/2 oz) tinned corn kernels,
drained
60 g (2¹/4 oz) thinly sliced ham, chopped
185 g (6¹/2 oz/1¹/2 cups) grated
cheddar cheese
100 g (3¹/2 oz/1 cup) grated
parmesan cheese
snipped chives, to garnish

SERVES 4–6

Put the pasta in a large heatproof bowl. Pour over boiling water and set aside, stirring occasionally, for 10 minutes. Drain.

Spray the slow cooker bowl with cooking oil spray or grease well with butter or oil.

Combine the evaporated milk, milk, egg and nutmeg in the slow cooker. Season with salt and freshly ground black pepper. Stir in the drained pasta, spring onion, corn, ham, 125 g (4¹/2 oz/1 cup) of the cheddar cheese and all of the parmesan cheese. Sprinkle over the remaining cheddar.

Cook on low for 2–3 hours. Take care not to overcook it – the sauce will still be a little wet in the centre. If cooked for too long, it will curdle, so start checking after 2 hours – the pasta should be *al dente* and the sauce thick. Spoon out onto serving plates, sprinkle with the chives and serve with a salad on the side.

PREPARATION TIME: 25 MINUTES   COOKING TIME: 2–3 HOURS

NOTE: Cook this recipe on low heat only. Leave out the ham for a vegetarian meal.

GREEK-STYLE STUFFED EGGPLANT

2 large eggplants (aubergines)
1 onion, finely chopped
2 garlic cloves, chopped
350 g (12 oz) minced (ground) lamb
60 g (2^1/$_4$ oz/^{1}/$_4$ cup) tomato paste
(concentrated purée)
185 ml (6 fl oz/^{3}/$_4$ cup) red wine
400 g (14 oz) tinned chopped tomatoes
250 ml (9 fl oz/1 cup) chicken stock
2 bay leaves
1 cinnamon stick
1 tablespoon dried oregano
Greek-style yoghurt, to serve

SERVES 4

Halve the eggplants lengthways. Use a sharp knife to cut a deep circle around the flesh, about 1 cm (^{1}/$_2$ inch) in from the edge. Use a large spoon to scoop out the eggplant flesh, then roughly chop the flesh.

Place the eggplant flesh in a bowl along with the onion, garlic, lamb and tomato paste. Season with salt and freshly ground black pepper and mix well to combine.

Stuff the mixture into the hole in the eggplants, reserving any left-over stuffing, and place the filled eggplants in the slow cooker. Pour over the wine, tomatoes and stock and add the bay leaves, cinnamon stick, oregano and any remaining eggplant stuffing. Cook on low for 6 hours, or until the eggplants are tender.

Remove the eggplants to a serving platter. Season to taste with salt and freshly ground black pepper. Serve topped with a dollop of yoghurt and a Greek salad on the side.

PREPARATION TIME: 20 MINUTES   COOKING TIME: 6 HOURS

April 2012
Ok, but not stellar
used 1 can evaporated milk

CREAMY TOMATO AND CHICKEN STEW

1.5 kg (3 lb 5 oz) chicken pieces, trimmed of excess fat

4 bacon slices, fat removed, roughly chopped

2 onions, chopped

1 garlic clove, crushed

400 g (14 oz) tinned chopped tomatoes

300 g (10 1/2 oz) small button mushrooms, halved

250 ml (9 fl oz/1 cup) pouring cream

2 tablespoons chopped flat-leaf (Italian) parsley

2 tablespoons lemon thyme

SERVES 4

Put the chicken, bacon, onion, garlic and tomatoes in the slow cooker. Cook on high for 3 hours, or until the chicken is nearly tender.

Add the mushrooms and cream and cook for a further 30 minutes, then remove the lid and cook for another 30 minutes to thicken the sauce. Stir through the parsley and lemon thyme. Serve with mashed potatoes and green beans.

PREPARATION TIME: 20 MINUTES   COOKING TIME: 4 HOURS

CHICKEN GOULASH

700 g (1 lb 9 oz) boneless, skinless chicken thighs

1 onion, sliced

2 garlic cloves, sliced

2 green capsicums (peppers), seeded and sliced

1 tablespoon sweet paprika

125 g (4 1/2 oz/1/2 cup) tomato passata (puréed tomatoes)

1 marjoram sprig

125 ml (4 fl oz/1/2 cup) white wine

250 ml (9 fl oz/1 cup) chicken stock

125 g (4 1/2 oz/1/2 cup) sour cream or crème fraîche

1 tablespoon cornflour (cornstarch)

1 small handful flat-leaf (Italian) parsley

SERVES 4

Trim the chicken of any fat and cut each thigh into quarters. Put the chicken pieces, onion, garlic, capsicum, paprika, tomato passata and marjoram in the slow cooker. Pour in the wine and stock. Cook on low for 4 1/2 hours, or until the chicken is tender.

Combine the sour cream and cornflour in a small bowl. Stir into the chicken mixture in the slow cooker. Cook for a further 5-10 minutes, or until thickened. Season to taste with salt and freshly ground black pepper, and stir through the parsley. Serve the goulash with rice.

PREPARATION TIME: 20 MINUTES   COOKING TIME: 4 3/4 HOURS

Creamy tomato and chicken stew

APRICOT CHICKEN

4 x 280 g (10 oz) boneless, skinless chicken breasts
1 garlic clove, crushed
1 tablespoon grated fresh ginger
1 tablespoon ground cumin
1 tablespoon ground coriander
1 teaspoon ground cinnamon
2 tablespoons vegetable oil
30 g (1 oz/^{1}/$_4$ cup) plain (all-purpose) flour
400 ml (14 fl oz) tinned apricot nectar
1 tablespoon honey
1 tablespoon lemon juice
60 g (2^1/$_4$ oz/^{1}/$_2$ cup) slivered almonds, toasted
1 handful coriander (cilantro) leaves

SERVES 4

Put the chicken, garlic, ginger, cumin, coriander, cinnamon and oil in a flat dish. Toss to thoroughly coat the chicken in the oil and spices. Cover and refrigerate overnight.

Put the flour in a flat dish. Remove the chicken from the marinade and dust with the flour. Place the chicken in the slow cooker with the apricot nectar, honey and lemon juice. Cook on high for 4 hours, or until the chicken is cooked through.

Season to taste with salt and freshly ground black pepper. Top with the toasted almonds and coriander and serve with rice.

PREPARATION TIME: 15 MINUTES +   COOKING TIME: 4 HOURS

CHICKEN CASSEROLE WITH MUSTARD AND TARRAGON

1 kg (2 lb 4 oz) boneless, skinless chicken thighs
1 onion, finely chopped
1 leek, white part only, thinly sliced
1 garlic clove, finely chopped
^{1}/$_2$ teaspoon dried tarragon
125 ml (4 fl oz/^{1}/$_2$ cup) chicken stock
350 g (12 oz) button mushrooms, sliced
185 ml (6 fl oz/^{3}/$_4$ cup) pouring cream
2 tablespoons dijon mustard
1^1/$_2$ tablespoons lemon juice

SERVES 4–6

Trim the chicken of any fat, then cut into quarters. Put the chicken pieces, onion, leek, garlic, tarragon and stock in the slow cooker. Cook on high for 2^1/$_2$ hours.

Add the mushrooms, cream and mustard. Stir to combine, then cook for a further 30 minutes. Stir through the lemon juice. Serve with mashed potatoes and zucchini or green beans.

PREPARATION TIME: 20 MINUTES   COOKING TIME: 3 HOURS

BASQUE CHICKEN

1.8 kg (4 lb) chicken (see Note)
1 onion, cut into 2 cm (^{3}/$_4$ inch) dice
1 red capsicum (pepper), cut into
2 cm (^{3}/$_4$ inch) dice
1 green capsicum (pepper), cut into
2 cm (^{3}/$_4$ inch) dice
2 garlic cloves, finely chopped
200 g (7 oz) chorizo sausage, sliced
150 ml (5 fl oz) white wine
80 g (2^3/$_4$ oz) tomato paste
(concentrated purée)
90 g (3^1/$_4$ oz/^{1}/$_2$ cup) black olives
^{1}/$_4$ preserved lemon
2 tablespoons chopped basil
2 tablespoons chopped flat-leaf
(Italian) parsley

SERVES 4

Joint the chicken into eight pieces by removing both legs and cutting between the joint of the drumstick and the thigh. Cut down either side of the backbone and lift it out. Turn the chicken over and cut through the cartilage down the centre of the breastbone. Cut each breast in half, leaving the wing attached to the top half.

Combine the chicken pieces, onion, red and green capsicum, garlic, chorizo, wine, tomato paste and olives in the slow cooker.

Rinse the preserved lemon well, remove and discard the pulp and membrane and finely dice the rind. Add to the chicken and cook on low for 8 hours, or until cooked through.

Stir through the basil and serve sprinkled with the parsley. Serve with rice if desired.

PREPARATION TIME: 25 MINUTES   COOKING TIME: 8 HOURS

NOTE: Alternatively, buy 1.8 kg (4 lb) chicken pieces

TURKEY POT ROAST

1.5 kg (3 lb 5 oz) frozen turkey breast roll
1 onion, cut into wedges
300 g (10^1/$_2$ oz) orange sweet potato, cut
into 3 cm (1^1/$_4$ inch) pieces
125 ml (4 fl oz/^{1}/$_2$ cup) white wine
125 ml (4 fl oz/^{1}/$_2$ cup) chicken stock
2 zucchini (courgettes), cut into
2 cm (^{3}/$_4$ inch) slices
160 g (5^1/$_2$ oz/^{1}/$_2$ cup) redcurrant jelly
1 tablespoon cornflour (cornstarch)

SERVES 6

Thaw the turkey according to the packet instructions. Remove the elastic string from the turkey and tie up securely with kitchen string, at regular intervals, to retain its shape.

Put the turkey in the slow cooker. Put the onion and sweet potato around the turkey, then pour over the wine and stock. Cook on low for 4 hours.

Add the zucchini and redcurrant jelly. Remove the lid, increase the heat to high and cook for a further 30 minutes. Transfer the turkey and vegetables to a plate, cover and keep warm.

Combine the cornflour and 1 tablespoon water in a small bowl and stir until smooth. Add the cornflour mixture to the slow cooker and cook, stirring, on high heat for about 10 minutes, or until the sauce thickens. Slice the turkey and serve with the vegetables and sauce.

PREPARATION TIME: 20 MINUTES   COOKING TIME: 4^3/$_4$ HOURS

CABBAGE ROLLS

½ large cabbage
400 g (14 oz) minced (ground) pork
220 g (7¾ oz/1 cup) par-cooked short-grain rice
50 g (1¾ oz/½ cup) seasoned stuffing mix or dry breadcrumbs
2 garlic cloves, crushed
1 egg, lightly beaten
1 onion, finely diced
1 tablespoon dijon mustard
1 tablespoon worcestershire sauce
¼ teaspoon white pepper
60 ml (2 fl oz/¼ cup) red wine vinegar
2 bacon slices, thinly sliced
500 g (1 lb 2 oz/2 cups) tomato passata (puréed tomatoes)

SERVES 4

Place the cabbage in a large heatproof bowl. Pour over boiling water to cover. Set aside for 5–10 minutes, or until you can separate the cabbage leaves with kitchen tongs. Refresh the leaves in cold water and drain.

Combine the pork, rice, stuffing mix, garlic, egg, onion, mustard, worcestershire sauce, white pepper and 1½ teaspoons salt in a bowl. Add 1 tablespoon of the vinegar.

Use the larger cabbage leaves to roll the parcels, and set the smaller leaves aside for later use. Cut a 'V' shape to remove the large connecting vein in each cabbage leaf. Form some of the pork stuffing mixture into a sausage shape about 2 cm (¾ inch) thick and 4 cm (1½ inches) long and place it in the middle of the cabbage leaf. Roll the cabbage up around the pork, making sure the filling is completely covered. Continue until all the large leaves are used.

Thinly shred the reserved small cabbage leaves and place them in the base of the slow cooker. Put the bacon on top, then the cabbage rolls. Top with the tomato passata and remaining vinegar. Cook on high for 2½ hours, or until the pork filling is cooked through.

PREPARATION TIME: 30 MINUTES   COOKING TIME: 2½ HOURS

LION'S HEAD MEATBALLS

450 g (1 lb) minced (ground) pork
1 egg white
4 spring onions (scallions), finely chopped
1 tablespoon Chinese rice wine
1 teaspoon grated fresh ginger
1 tablespoon light soy sauce
2 teaspoons sugar
1 teaspoon sesame oil
white pepper
750 ml (26 fl oz/3 cups) chicken stock
300 g (10^1/$_2$ oz) bok choy (pak choy), sliced
100 g (3^1/$_2$ oz) dried rice vermicelli noodles

SERVES 4

Put the pork and egg white in a food processor and process briefly until you have a fluffy mixture. Alternatively mash the pork in a large bowl and gradually stir in the egg white, beating the mixture well until it is fluffy.

Add the spring onion, rice wine, ginger, soy sauce, sugar and sesame oil, season with salt and white pepper, and process or beat again briefly. Divide the mixture into walnut-sized balls.

Place the meatballs in the slow cooker, then pour in the stock. Cook on low for 2 hours. Add the bok choy and cook for a further 10 minutes, or until the bok choy is wilted.

Meanwhile, place the vermicelli noodles in a heatproof bowl, cover with boiling water and soak for 10 minutes, or until soft. Drain the vermicelli and add them to the slow cooker. Stir to combine. To serve, ladle the vermicelli, meatballs and some broth into deep bowls.

PREPARATION TIME: 30 MINUTES   COOKING TIME: 2^1/$_4$ HOURS

PORK SAUSAGES CASSOULET

8 thin pork sausages
1 onion, cut into thin wedges
180 g (6^1/$_4$ oz) mushrooms, sliced
2 garlic cloves, chopped
1 teaspoon paprika
400 g (14 oz) tinned chopped tomatoes
1 tablespoon tomato paste (concentrated purée)
1 tablespoon seeded mustard
400 g (14 oz) tinned butter or red kidney beans, drained and rinsed
2 tablespoons chopped flat-leaf (Italian) parsley

SERVES 4

Prick the sausages all over and put into the slow cooker. Add the onion, mushrooms and garlic and sprinkle over the paprika, salt and freshly ground black pepper. Pour over the tomatoes, tomato paste and mustard.

Cook on high for 3 hours, or until the sausages are cooked through. Stir in the beans and cook for a further 15 minutes, or until the beans are heated through. Scatter with parsley before serving.

PREPARATION TIME: 15 MINUTES   COOKING TIME: 3^1/$_4$ HOURS

NOTE: You can brown off the sausages in a non-stick frying pan before adding them to the slow cooker if preferred.

SPARE RIBS WITH BEER AND BARBECUE SAUCE

1.5 kg (3 lb 5 oz) pork spare ribs
185 ml (6 fl oz/¾ cup) beer
185 ml (6 fl oz/¾ cup) barbecue sauce
2 tablespoons sweet chilli sauce
1 tablespoon worcestershire sauce
1 tablespoon honey
2 spring onions (scallions), thinly sliced
2 garlic cloves, crushed
1 tablespoon cornflour (cornstarch)
1 small handful coriander (cilantro) leaves,
to garnish

SERVES 4–6

Cut the ribs into individual ribs, or into sets of two or three if preferred, and trim away any excess fat.

In a large bowl, combine the beer, barbecue sauce, sweet chilli sauce, worcestershire sauce, honey, spring onion and garlic. Season with salt and freshly ground black pepper. Add the ribs and thoroughly coat them in the sauce.

Transfer the ribs and the marinade to the slow cooker. Cook on high for 4–5 hours. After 4 hours, check to see if the ribs are tender but the meat should not be falling off the bone. If necessary, continue to cook for the extra hour.

Using kitchen tongs, remove the ribs to a side plate and cover to keep warm. Mix the cornflour with 1 tablespoon water and stir into the sauce in the slow cooker. Cook on high heat for 5–10 minutes, stirring, or until the sauce has thickened.

Serve the ribs piled onto plates and spoon over some of the sauce. Sprinkle over the coriander leaves. Supply lots of paper napkins for sticky fingers.

PREPARATION TIME: 20 MINUTES   COOKING TIME: 4–5 HOURS

SPANISH-STYLE PORK AND VEGETABLE STEW

1 kg (2 lb 4 oz) boneless pork shoulder
2 hot chorizo sausages, sliced
600 g (1 lb 5 oz) all-purpose potatoes, cubed
1 red onion, diced
2 garlic cloves, chopped
2 red capsicums (peppers), seeded and chopped
400 g (14 oz) tinned chopped tomatoes
pinch saffron threads
1 tablespoon sweet paprika
10 large thyme sprigs
1 bay leaf
60 g (2^1/$_4$ oz/^{1}/$_4$ cup) tomato paste (concentrated purée)
125 ml (4 fl oz/^{1}/$_2$ cup) white wine
125 ml (4 fl oz/^{1}/$_2$ cup) chicken stock
2 tablespoons sherry
1 handful flat-leaf (Italian) parsley, chopped

SERVES 4–6

Trim the pork and cut into 4 cm (1^1/$_2$ inch) cubes. Put the pork, chorizo, potato, onion, garlic, capsicum, tomatoes, saffron, paprika, thyme and bay leaf in the slow cooker.

Combine the tomato paste, wine, stock and sherry in a small bowl and pour over the pork and vegetables. Cook on high for 4 hours, or until the pork is tender.

Season to taste with salt and freshly ground black pepper. Stir through the parsley and serve.

PREPARATION TIME: 25 MINUTES   COOKING TIME: 4 HOURS

SWEET PAPRIKA VEAL GOULASH

1 kg (2 lb 4 oz) boneless veal shoulder
1 onion, sliced
2 garlic cloves, crushed
1 tablespoon sweet paprika
1/2 teaspoon caraway seeds
2 bay leaves
625 g (1 lb 6 oz/2 1/2 cups) tomato passata (puréed tomatoes)
125 ml (4 fl oz/ 1/2 cup) chicken stock
125 ml (4 fl oz/ 1/2 cup) red wine
2 all-purpose potatoes, diced
275 g (9 3/4 oz) jar roasted red capsicums (peppers), drained and rinsed
sour cream, to serve

SERVES 4

Cut the veal into 3 cm (1 1/4 inch) cubes. Put the veal, onion, garlic, paprika, caraway seeds, bay leaves, tomato passata, stock, red wine and potatoes in the slow cooker. Cook on high for 4 hours, or until the veal is tender. Stir through the capsicum and cook for a further 5 minutes, or until warmed through.

Taste and season with salt and freshly ground black pepper. Serve with a dollop of sour cream and with cooked fettuccine noodles.

PREPARATION TIME: 20 MINUTES   COOKING TIME: 4 HOURS

VEAL WITH SWEET POTATO, TOMATO AND OLIVES

1 kg (2 lb 4 oz) piece veal (rump)
350 g (12 oz) orange sweet potato
1 large red onion, chopped
1 celery stalk, chopped
2 garlic cloves, chopped
400 g (14 oz) tinned chopped tomatoes
60 ml (2 fl oz/ 1/4 cup) white wine or water
2 tablespoons tomato paste (concentrated purée)
1 rosemary sprig
1 tablespoon cornflour (cornstarch)
12 pitted or stuffed green olives
2 tablespoons chopped parsley
grated zest of 1 small lemon

SERVES 4

Cut the veal into 4 cm (1 1/2 inch) cubes. Peel the sweet potato and cut into 4 cm (1 1/2 inch) cubes.

Put the veal, sweet potato, onion, celery, garlic, tomatoes, wine, tomato paste and rosemary in the slow cooker. Season with salt and freshly ground black pepper. Cook on high for 4 hours, or until the veal is tender and cooked through. Remove the rosemary sprig.

Combine the cornflour with a little water to make a smooth paste and stir it into the veal. Cook for a further 5-10 minutes to thicken the juices a little. Stir through the olives and sprinkle with the chopped parsley and lemon zest to serve.

PREPARATION TIME: 15 MINUTES   COOKING TIME: 4 1/4 HOURS

ITALIAN BEEF CASSEROLE WITH DUMPLINGS

1 kg (2 lb 4 oz) chuck, blade or skirt steak

1 onion, sliced

2 garlic cloves, crushed

250 ml (9 fl oz/1 cup) beef stock

2 x 425 g (15 oz) tins chopped tomatoes

450 g (1 lb) jar roasted red capsicums (peppers), drained and thickly sliced

1 tablespoon chopped oregano

90 g ($3^1/4$ oz/$^1/3$ cup) ready-made pesto, to serve

DUMPLINGS

40 g ($1^1/2$ oz/$^1/3$ cup) plain (all-purpose) flour

35 g ($1^1/4$ oz/$^1/4$ cup) polenta

1 teaspoon baking powder

1 egg white

2 tablespoons milk

1 tablespoon olive oil

SERVES 4–6

Trim the beef and cut into 3 cm ($1^1/4$ inch) cubes. Put the beef cubes, onion, garlic, stock, tomatoes, capsicum and oregano in the slow cooker. Season with salt and freshly ground black pepper. Cook on high for 4 hours, or until the beef is tender.

To make the dumplings, combine the flour, polenta, baking powder and $^1/2$ teaspoon salt in a large bowl. Make a well in the centre and add the egg white, milk and olive oil. Stir well to combine. Using teaspoonfuls of the polenta mixture, form it into small balls. Add the dumplings to the slow cooker and cook for a further 30 minutes, or until the dumplings are cooked through.

Check the seasoning and add extra salt and pepper if needed. Serve the casserole and dumplings topped with a dollop of pesto.

PREPARATION TIME: 30 MINUTES   COOKING TIME: $4^1/2$ HOURS

CURRIED SAUSAGES WITH POTATOES AND PEAS

1 tablespoon red lentils
1 teaspoon black peppercorns
1 small dried red chilli, roughly chopped
$1/2$ teaspoon cumin seeds
$1/2$ teaspoon coriander seeds
3 all-purpose potatoes, cut into
3 cm ($1^1/4$ inch) pieces
1 onion, thickly sliced
500 g (1 lb 2 oz) beef or pork sausages
2 fresh curry leaves (optional)
2 tablespoons brandy
60 ml (2 fl oz/$^1/4$ cup) beef stock
1 tablespoon dijon mustard
100 ml ($3^1/2$ fl oz) pouring cream
155 g ($5^1/2$ oz/1 cup) fresh or frozen peas
1 handful flat-leaf (Italian) parsley,
chopped
tomato relish, to serve

SERVES 4

Using a mortar and pestle or spice grinder, pound or grind the lentils, peppercorns, chilli, cumin seeds and coriander seeds to a fine powder. Push the powder through a fine strainer and set aside.

Put the potato and onion in the base of the slow cooker and top with the sausages and curry leaves, if using. Combine the brandy, beef stock, mustard and cream and pour over the sausages. Cook on low for 4 hours, or until the sausages are cooked through. Stir in the peas and cook for a further 5 minutes, or until the peas are tender.

Season to taste with salt and freshly ground black pepper. Stir through the parsley and serve with tomato relish.

PREPARATION TIME: 20 MINUTES   COOKING TIME: 4 HOURS

COUNTRY BEEF STEW

1 kg (2 lb 4 oz) chuck, blade or skirt steak

1 small eggplant (aubergine), cut into 1.5 cm (^{5}/8 inch) cubes

250 g (9 oz) baby new potatoes, halved

2 celery stalks, sliced

3 carrots, chopped

2 red onions, sliced

6 ripe tomatoes, chopped

2 garlic cloves, crushed

1 teaspoon ground coriander

^{1}/2 teaspoon allspice

^{3}/4 teaspoon sweet paprika

250 ml (9 fl oz/1 cup) red wine

500 ml (17 fl oz/2 cups) beef stock

2 tablespoons tomato paste (concentrated purée)

2 bay leaves

3 tablespoons flat-leaf (Italian) parsley, chopped

SERVES 6–8

Trim the beef and cut it into 4 cm (1^1/2 inch) cubes. Put the beef in the slow cooker along with the eggplant, potato, celery, carrot, onion, tomato, garlic, coriander, allspice, paprika, wine, stock, tomato paste and bay leaves. Cook on low for 5^1/2 hours, or until the beef is tender and cooked through.

Season to taste with salt and freshly ground black pepper. Stir through the parsley and serve.

PREPARATION TIME: 30 MINUTES   COOKING TIME: 5^1/2 HOURS

MINTED BEEF AND TURNIP STEW

1 kg (2 lb 4 oz) chuck steak

2 onions, thinly sliced

4 small turnips, cut into wedges

150 g (5^1/2 oz) bacon slices, diced

125 ml (4 fl oz/^{1}/2 cup) red wine

1^1/2 tablespoons red wine vinegar

250 ml (9 fl oz/1 cup) beef stock

1 large mint sprig

SERVES 4–6

Trim the beef and cut it into 4 cm (1^1/2 inch) cubes. Put the beef, onion, turnip, bacon, wine, vinegar, stock and mint in the slow cooker. Cook on low for 4 hours, or until the beef is tender.

Remove the mint sprig. Season to taste with salt and freshly ground black pepper and serve with crusty bread.

PREPARATION TIME: 15 MINUTES   COOKING TIME: 4 HOURS

Country beef stew

ITALIAN MEATBALLS WITH TOMATO SAUCE

MEATBALLS
1 onion, finely chopped
80 g (2³/4 oz/¹/2 cup) pine nuts, roughly chopped
2 garlic cloves, crushed
1 small handful flat-leaf (Italian) parsley, roughly chopped
1 teaspoon chopped rosemary
2 teaspoons fennel seeds, ground
55 g (2 oz/²/3 cup) fresh breadcrumbs
25 g (1 oz/¹/4 cup) freshly grated parmesan cheese
grated zest of 1 large lemon
1 egg
500 g (1 lb 2 oz) minced (ground) pork or beef

700 g (1 lb 9 oz) tomato passata (puréed tomatoes)
125 ml (4 fl oz/¹/2 cup) red wine

SERVES 4–6

To make the meatballs, combine all the ingredients in a bowl. Use your hands to mix well. Roll the mixture into walnut-sized balls and place on a tray. Refrigerate the meatballs for 20 minutes.

Put the tomato passata, wine and meatballs in the slow cooker. Season with salt and freshly ground black pepper and cook on high for 4 hours, or until the meatballs are cooked through and tender.

Serve the meatballs and tomato sauce with spaghetti, rice or mashed potatoes, and a side salad.

PREPARATION TIME: 25 MINUTES   COOKING TIME: 4 HOURS

BRAISED BEEF SHORT RIBS

2 kg (4 lb 8 oz) beef short ribs
180 g (6^1/$_2$ oz) bacon slices
2 onions, chopped
1 garlic clove, crushed
1 small red chilli, seeded and thinly sliced
500 ml (17 fl oz/2 cups) beef stock
400 g (14 oz) tinned chopped tomatoes
8 bulb spring onions (scallions), trimmed
and leaves removed
2 strips lemon zest, white pith removed
1 teaspoon mild paprika
1 teaspoon chopped rosemary
1 bay leaf
1 tablespoon soft brown sugar
1 teaspoon worcestershire sauce
2 tablespoons chopped basil
2 tablespoons chopped flat-leaf
(Italian) parsley

SERVES 6

Chop the ribs into 4 cm (1^1/$_2$ inch) lengths. Remove the rind and fat from the bacon and cut into 5 mm (^{1}/$_4$ inch) dice.

Put the ribs, bacon, onion, garlic, chilli, stock, tomatoes, spring onions, strips of lemon zest, paprika, rosemary, bay leaf, brown sugar and worcestershire sauce in the slow cooker. Cook on high for 4–5 hours, or until the ribs are tender.

Skim off as much fat as you can from the top. Stir through the basil and parsley. Serve the ribs with mashed potatoes or soft polenta if desired.

PREPARATION TIME: 15 MINUTES   COOKING TIME: 4–5 HOURS

BEEF CARBONNADE

1.2 kg (2 lb 10 oz) chuck steak
3 onions, chopped
1 garlic clove, crushed
1 teaspoon soft brown sugar
375 ml (13 fl oz/1^1/$_2$ cups) beer
(bitter or stout)
2 bay leaves
4 thyme sprigs
2 tablespoons plain (all-purpose) flour
1 handful flat-leaf (Italian) parsley,
chopped

SERVES 4

Trim the beef of excess fat and cut into 4 cm (1^1/$_2$ inch) cubes. Put the beef, onion, garlic, brown sugar, beer, bay leaves, thyme and flour in the slow cooker and stir to combine. Season with freshly ground black pepper. Cook on high for 4 hours, or until the beef is cooked through.

Season to taste with salt and extra pepper if desired, and sprinkle with the parsley. Serve with green beans or zucchini.

PREPARATION TIME: 15 MINUTES   COOKING TIME: 4 HOURS

Braised beef short ribs

CORNED BEEF WITH CABBAGE AND POTATOES

1.5 kg (3 lb 5 oz) piece corned beef
(silverside)
1 small onion
8 whole cloves
500 g (1 lb 2 oz) small new potatoes
(about 12)
1 tablespoon soft brown sugar
1 tablespoon malt vinegar
8 black peppercorns
2 bay leaves
500 g (1 lb 2 oz) savoy cabbage, core
attached and cut into 4-6 wedges

MUSTARD AND PARSLEY SAUCE
1 egg
2 tablespoons caster (superfine) sugar
1 tablespoon plain (all-purpose) flour
1 teaspoon mustard powder
60 ml (2 fl oz/$\frac{1}{4}$ cup) malt vinegar
2 tablespoons finely chopped flat-leaf
(Italian) parsley

SERVES 4-6

Rinse the corned beef, pat dry with paper towel and then trim off any excess fat. Peel the onion and stud it with the cloves.

Put the potatoes in the slow cooker in a single layer and top with the corned beef. Barely cover with cold water. Add the onion, the combined brown sugar and malt vinegar, the peppercorns and bay leaves.

Cook on low for 8-10 hours, or until the beef is tender. About 45 minutes before the end of cooking time, arrange the cabbage wedges around the meat, cover and cook until the cabbage is tender. When the beef is cooked, remove to a side plate and cover with foil to keep warm.

To make the mustard and parsley sauce, remove 250 ml (9 fl oz/1 cup) of the cooking liquid from the slow cooker and set aside. Whisk together the egg and sugar in a small bowl, then whisk in the flour and mustard powder. Gradually add the reserved cooking liquid and the vinegar, mixing until smooth. Pour into a small saucepan and stir over medium heat until thickened. Stir through the parsley.

To serve, cut the corned beef into thick slices. Use a slotted spoon to lift the potatoes and cabbage out of the slow cooker to the serving plates. Discard the onion. Serve with the mustard and parsley sauce and with some steamed carrots and green beans if desired.

PREPARATION TIME: 20 MINUTES   COOKING TIME: 8-10 HOURS

NOTE: Store left-over corned beef in a bowl with the remaining cooking liquid to cover. Cover with plastic wrap and refrigerate.

Aug 29/09
First cool day at the end of the summer. So pulled out the slow cooker
for the 1st time in months! Excellent stew!

STIFATHO

1 kg (2 lb 4 oz) chuck steak
500 g (1 lb 2 oz) whole baby onions
1 garlic clove, cut in half lengthways
125 ml (4 fl oz/$1/2$ cup) red wine
125 ml (4 fl oz/$1/2$ cup) beef stock
1 cinnamon stick
4 whole cloves
1 bay leaf
1 tablespoon red wine vinegar
2 tablespoons tomato paste
(concentrated purée)
2 tablespoons currants

SERVES 4

Trim the beef of excess fat and sinew, then cut into 5 cm (2 inch) cubes. Put the beef, onions, garlic, wine, stock, cinnamon stick, cloves, bay leaf, vinegar, tomato paste and some freshly ground black pepper in the slow cooker. Cook on high for 4 hours.

Stir through the currants and cook for a further 15 minutes. Discard the cinnamon stick and season to taste with salt and extra pepper. Serve with rice, bread or potatoes.

PREPARATION TIME: 20 MINUTES   COOKING TIME: 4$1/4$ HOURS

PORCUPINE MEATBALLS

500 g (1 lb 2 oz) minced (ground) beef
220 g (7$3/4$ oz/1 cup) short-grain rice
1 onion, chopped
1 teaspoon freshly grated nutmeg
2 bay leaves
80 ml (2$1/2$ fl oz/$1/3$ cup) worcestershire
sauce
420 g (15 oz) tinned tomato soup

MAKES 40 MEATBALLS

Combine the beef, rice, onion and nutmeg in a bowl and season with salt and freshly ground black pepper. Using about 1$1/2$ tablespoons of beef mixture for each, roll the mixture into balls. Cover and chill in the refrigerator overnight.

Put the meatballs and bay leaves in the slow cooker and cover with the combined worcestershire sauce and tomato soup. Cook on low for 3 hours, or until the meatballs are cooked through.

Taste the sauce and adjust the seasoning if necessary. Serve with steamed vegetables.

PREPARATION TIME: 10 MINUTES +   COOKING TIME: 3 HOURS

MEATLOAF WITH TOMATO SAUCE GLAZE

TOMATO SAUCE GLAZE
250 g (9 oz/1 cup) tomato sauce (ketchup)
2 tablespoons tomato chutney
1 tablespoon soft brown sugar
2 teaspoons worcestershire sauce
1 teaspoon mustard powder

MEATLOAF
1 carrot, diced
1 celery stalk, diced
1 red or green capsicum (pepper), seeded
and diced
4 spring onions (scallions), chopped
155 g (5$^1/_2$ oz/1 cup) fresh or frozen peas
1 kg (2 lb 4 oz) minced (ground) beef
1 teaspoon dried oregano
2 slices wholegrain bread, crusts
removed, diced
2 eggs, lightly beaten
cooking oil spray

SERVES 4–6

To make the tomato sauce glaze, combine the tomato sauce, chutney, brown sugar, worcestershire sauce and mustard in a small bowl. Set aside.

To make the meatloaf, combine the carrot, celery, capsicum, spring onion and peas in a large bowl, then add the beef, oregano and diced bread. Season well with salt and freshly ground black pepper. Using clean hands, thoroughly combine the mixture.

Add about a quarter of the tomato sauce glaze to the beef mixture along with the beaten egg and thoroughly mix again. Set aside the remaining tomato sauce glaze.

Spray the slow cooker bowl with cooking oil spray or lightly grease with butter or oil. Cut a sheet of foil long enough to fit across the base and up both sides of the bowl, fold it into four lengthways and place across the centre of the bowl.

Press the beef mixture evenly into the slow cooker bowl and smooth the surface. Fold down the foil ends if necessary so the lid can be placed on securely. Cover with the lid and cook on low for 5–6 hours, or until the meatloaf is cooked through and has left the side of the bowl.

To serve, use the foil 'handles' to carefully lift the meatloaf onto a serving plate. Heat the reserved tomato sauce glaze in the slow cooker and pour over the meatloaf. Cut into thick slices and serve with mashed sweet potato and a green salad.

PREPARATION TIME: 30 MINUTES   COOKING TIME: 5–6 HOURS

GREEK LAMB WITH MACARONI

1 kg (2 lb 4 oz) boneless lamb leg
1 large onion, chopped
2 garlic cloves, crushed
400 g (14 oz) tinned chopped tomatoes
60 g (2¼ oz/¼ cup) tomato paste
(concentrated purée)
500 ml (17 fl oz/2 cups) beef stock
2 tablespoons red wine vinegar
1 tablespoon soft brown sugar
1 teaspoon dried oregano
200 g (7 oz/2 cups) macaroni pasta
125 g (4½ oz) pecorino cheese, grated

SERVES 4–6

Trim the lamb of any excess fat and cut into 3 cm (1¼ inch) cubes. Put the lamb, onion, garlic, tomatoes, tomato paste, stock, vinegar, brown sugar and oregano in the slow cooker. Cook on high for 1³/₄ hours, or until the lamb is tender.

Place the macaroni in a large heatproof bowl and cover with boiling water. Set aside for 10 minutes. Drain and add the macaroni to the slow cooker and stir to combine. Cook for a further 30 minutes, or until the pasta is tender and the liquid has absorbed.

Divide among serving bowls and sprinkle with the cheese.

PREPARATION TIME: 30 MINUTES   COOKING TIME: 2¼ HOURS

BRAISED LAMB WITH CAPSICUM AND FENNEL

1 kg (2 lb 4 oz) lamb shoulder or leg
1 large onion, chopped
1 red capsicum (pepper), seeded and
sliced into strips
1 yellow capsicum (pepper), seeded and
sliced into strips
2 fennel bulbs, trimmed and each cut
into thick slices lengthways
4 garlic cloves, chopped
250 ml (9 fl oz/1 cup) tomato passata
(puréed tomatoes)
60 ml (2 fl oz/¼ cup) beef stock or water
1 tablespoon tomato paste
(concentrated purée)
1 teaspoon worcestershire sauce
1 tablespoon cornflour (cornstarch)
fennel fronds, to garnish

SERVES 4

Trim the lamb of any excess fat and cut into 4 cm (1½ inch) cubes. Put the lamb, onion, red and yellow capsicum, fennel, garlic, tomato passata, stock, tomato paste and worcestershire sauce in the slow cooker. Season with salt and freshly ground black pepper. Cook on high for 4 hours, or until the lamb is tender and cooked through.

Combine the cornflour with a little water to make a smooth paste and stir it into the lamb. Cook for a further 5-10 minutes to thicken the juices a little.

To serve, divide the lamb among the serving bowls and scatter over some chopped fennel fronds.

PREPARATION TIME: 15 MINUTES   COOKING TIME: 4¼ HOURS

LANCASHIRE HOTPOT

4 all-purpose potatoes, sliced
6 baby onions, peeled and left whole
1 tablespoon thyme, chopped
1 kg (2 lb 4 oz) lamb shoulder chops
2 tablespoons worcestershire sauce
125 ml (4 fl oz/^{1}/$_2$ cup) beef stock
1 handful flat-leaf (Italian) parsley,
chopped

SERVES 4

In a large bowl, toss together the potato, onions and thyme. Layer the potato and onions in the base of the slow cooker and top with the lamb chops. Pour over the worcestershire sauce and stock. Cook on high for 4 hours, or until the lamb is tender and cooked through.

Season with salt and freshly ground black pepper, and stir through the parsley before serving.

PREPARATION TIME: 15 MINUTES   COOKING TIME: 4 HOURS

GREEK LEG OF LAMB WITH OREGANO

1.8 kg (4 lb) lamb leg
1 tablespoon dried oregano
8 small all-purpose potatoes, such as coliban, peeled and halved
400 g (14 oz) tinned chopped tomatoes
80 ml (2^1/$_2$ fl oz/^{1}/$_3$ cup) red wine
250 ml (9 fl oz/1 cup) chicken stock
1 strip lemon zest, white pith removed
2 bay leaves
1 tablespoon lemon juice
2 tablespoons chopped fresh oregano

SERVES 6

Put the lamb leg in the slow cooker and sprinkle with the dried oregano. Scatter the potatoes around the lamb. Add the tomatoes, wine, stock and 250 ml (9 fl oz/1 cup) water. Season with freshly ground black pepper and add the strip of lemon zest and the bay leaves. Cook on low for 10 hours, or until the lamb is cooked through.

Remove the lamb and potatoes and transfer to a platter. Skim the fat from the surface of the sauce and stir through the lemon juice and fresh oregano. Season the sauce with salt and freshly ground black pepper, then pour it over the lamb to serve.

PREPARATION TIME: 15 MINUTES   COOKING TIME: 10 HOURS

LAMB CHOPS IN RATATOUILLE

1 kg (2 lb 4 oz) lamb forequarter chops

1 eggplant (aubergine), cut into 2 cm (3/4 inch) cubes

1 red capsicum (pepper), cut into 2 cm (3/4 inch) cubes

1 green capsicum (pepper), cut into 2 cm (3/4 inch) cubes

1 red onion, cut into 1 cm (1/2 inch) cubes

2 tablespoons capers

4 anchovies, chopped

80 g (2 3/4 oz/1/2 cup) pitted kalamata olives, chopped

60 g (2 1/4 oz/1/4 cup) tomato paste (concentrated purée)

2 garlic cloves, chopped

400 g (14 oz) tinned chopped tomatoes

150 g (5 1/2 oz/3/4 cup) Israeli couscous (see Note)

1 small handful flat-leaf (Italian) parsley, chopped

SERVES 4–6

Trim the lamb chops of excess fat and cut into pieces. Put the eggplant, red and green capsicum, onion, capers, anchovies, olives, tomato paste, garlic and tomatoes in the slow cooker. Put the lamb chops on top. Cook on low for 6–6 1/2 hours, or until the lamb is tender, stirring occasionally.

Stir in the couscous and continue to cook for another 1 hour, or until the couscous is tender and cooked through.

Season with salt and freshly ground black pepper, and sprinkle with parsley before serving.

PREPARATION TIME: 30 MINUTES   COOKING TIME: 7–7 1/2 HOURS

NOTE: Israeli couscous is larger in size than the more familiar Moroccan couscous, and has a chewier texture. It is sold in most gourmet food stores and health food stores.

CHUTNEY CHOPS WITH POTATOES AND PEAS

1.2 kg (2 lb 10 oz) lamb forequarter chops
4 all-purpose potatoes, such as
desiree, sliced
2 garlic cloves, crushed
240 g (8¹/₂ oz) jar tomato fruit chutney
400 g (14 oz) tinned chopped tomatoes
125 ml (4 fl oz/¹/₂ cup) red wine
125 ml (4 fl oz/¹/₂ cup) chicken stock
2 rosemary sprigs
80 g (2³/₄ oz/¹/₂ cup) fresh or
frozen peas

SERVES 4

Trim the lamb chops of excess fat. Layer the chops and potato slices in the slow cooker.

Combine the garlic, chutney, tomatoes, wine, stock and rosemary and add to the slow cooker. Cook on high for 4 hours, or until the potato is tender and the meat is falling from the bones.

Stir through the peas and cook for a further 5 minutes. Season to taste with salt and freshly ground black pepper before serving.

PREPARATION TIME: 15 MINUTES   COOKING TIME: 4 HOURS

IRISH STEW

600 g (1 lb 5 oz) all-purpose potatoes,
thickly sliced
3 carrots, thickly sliced
1 onion, cut into 16 wedges
1 small leek, white part only,
thickly sliced
150 g (5¹/₂ oz) savoy cabbage, thinly
sliced
4 bacon slices, cut into strips
8 lamb neck chops
375 ml (13 fl oz/1¹/₂ cups) beef stock
2 tablespoons finely chopped flat-leaf
(Italian) parsley

SERVES 6

Layer half the potato, carrot, onion, leek, cabbage and bacon in the base of the slow cooker. Arrange the lamb chops in a single layer over the bacon and cover with layers of the remaining vegetables and bacon. Pour over the stock and cook on low for 4¹/₂ hours, or until the lamb is very tender and the sauce is slightly reduced.

Taste and check for seasoning. Divide among shallow bowls and sprinkle with the parsley. Serve with bread to mop up the juices.

PREPARATION TIME: 25 MINUTES   COOKING TIME: 4¹/₂ HOURS

Chutney chops with potatoes and peas

CRYING LEG OF LAMB

GARLIC RUB
2-3 garlic cloves, crushed
1 tablespoon olive oil
1 teaspoon dried oregano

4 all-purpose potatoes, halved
250 g (9 oz) orange sweet potato, cut into 5 cm (2 inch) chunks
150 g (5½ oz) long, thin eggplants (aubergines), cut into 5 cm (2 inch) chunks
2 tomatoes, quartered
1.5 kg (3 lb 5 oz) easy-carve lamb leg
1 tablespoon cornflour (cornstarch)

SERVES 4

To make the garlic rub, mash together the garlic and 1 teaspoon salt in a small bowl to make a paste. Stir in the olive oil and oregano and season with plenty of freshly ground black pepper.

Scatter the potato, sweet potato, eggplant and tomatoes over the base of the slow cooker.

Wash and pat dry the lamb with paper towel, and remove any excess fat. Rub the garlic paste all over the lamb. Place the lamb in the slow cooker on top of the vegetables. Cover and cook on low for 5-6 hours, or until the lamb is cooked to your liking.

Transfer the lamb to a large plate, cover with foil and leave to rest for 10 minutes. Use a slotted spoon to lift the vegetables from the juice to a serving plate.

Discard the fat from the surface of the juice left in the slow cooker. Increase the heat to high. Combine the cornflour with 1 tablespoon water and stir it into the juices. Stir over high heat for 10-15 minutes, or until thickened, then strain into a jug. Carve the lamb into thick chunks and serve with the vegetables and thickened juices.

PREPARATION TIME: 30 MINUTES   COOKING TIME: 5-6 HOURS

ENTERTAINING

SEAFOOD FIDEOS

300 g (10^1/$_2$ oz) raw prawns (shrimp)
300 g (10^1/$_2$ oz) firm white fish fillets
200 g (7 oz) squid tubes
1 kg (2 lb 4 oz) mussels
1 onion, finely chopped
1 garlic clove, finely chopped
400 g (14 oz) tinned whole tomatoes, strained (use juice only)
^{1}/$_2$ teaspoon chilli flakes
2 tablespoons chopped oregano
125 g (4^1/$_2$ oz) fideos or vermicelli pasta (see Note)
chopped flat-leaf (Italian) parsley, to serve
flour tortillas, to serve

SERVES 4–6

Prepare the seafood. Peel the prawns, leaving the heads and tails intact. Gently pull out the dark vein from each prawn back, starting at the head end. Cut the fish into 3 cm (1^1/$_4$ inch) pieces. Cut the squid tubes into 1 cm (^{1}/$_2$ inch) rings. Scrub the mussels with a stiff brush and pull out the hairy beards. Discard any broken mussels or open ones that don't close when tapped on the work surface.

Put the prepared prawns, fish, squid rings, mussels, onion, garlic, tomato juice, chilli and oregano in the slow cooker. Cook on high for 2 hours.

Break the noodles into 5 cm (2 inch) lengths. Place the noodles in a large heatproof bowl and cover with boiling water. Set aside to soften for 10 minutes, then drain.

Place the softened noodles on top of the seafood in the slow cooker. Cook for 1 hour on low. Transfer the seafood and noodles to a serving dish and sprinkle with chopped parsley. Serve with warmed flour tortillas.

PREPARATION TIME: 30 MINUTES   COOKING TIME: 3 HOURS

NOTE: Fideos is a traditional Mexican or Spanish dish. The word refers to the noodle that is used, which is a very thin, vermicelli-like pasta. If you can't find fideos noodles, use vermicelli or capellini pasta.

SALMON WITH HORSERADISH CRUST AND PUY LENTILS

400 g (14 oz/2 cups) puy lentils or tiny
blue-green lentils
500 ml (17 fl oz/2 cups) vegetable stock
grated zest and juice of 1 lemon
1 small green chilli, finely chopped
80 g (2³/4 oz/1 cup) fresh sourdough
breadcrumbs
2 tablespoons grated fresh or prepared
horseradish
4 tablespoons chopped dill
10 g (¹/4 oz) butter, melted
4 x 180 g (6¹/2 oz) salmon fillets
50 g (1³/4 oz) English spinach,
stalks removed, chopped
1 handful coriander (cilantro) leaves
125 g (4¹/2 oz/¹/2 cup) plain yoghurt,
to serve
lemon wedges, to serve

SERVES 4

Put the lentils, stock, lemon zest, lemon juice and chilli in the slow cooker. Cook on high for 3 hours.

In a food processor, roughly pulse the breadcrumbs and horseradish until well combined. Stir through the dill and melted butter until the mixture is fairly moist.

Remove any bones from the salmon using your fingers or tweezers, then press the breadcrumb mixture over the top side of the salmon fillets.

In a large non-stick frying pan over medium heat, cook the crumbed side of the salmon for 3 minutes, or until the crumbs are golden. Work in batches if necessary.

Mix the spinach through the lentils in the slow cooker and place the salmon on top. Cook on low for 1 hour, or until the fish is cooked through and flakes when tested with a fork. Remove the salmon to serving plates.

Mix the coriander through the lentils and spoon some lentils onto each plate. Serve the salmon topped with the yoghurt and with lemon wedges on the side.

PREPARATION TIME: 25 MINUTES   COOKING TIME: 4¹/4 HOURS

ZARZUELA

250 ml (9 fl oz/1 cup) dry white wine
large pinch saffron threads
3 garlic cloves, thinly sliced
1 leek, white part only, thinly sliced
1 red capsicum (pepper), seeded and
thinly sliced
1 green capsicum (pepper), seeded and
thinly sliced
2 teaspoons paprika
400 g (14 oz) tinned chopped tomatoes
20 g (3/4 oz) blanched almonds, finely
chopped
1 bay leaf
1 small red chilli, seeded and chopped
60 ml (2 fl oz/1/4 cup) brandy or cognac
2 tablespoons lemon juice
1.5 litres (52 fl oz/6 cups) fish or
chicken stock
500 g (1 lb 2 oz) skinless firm white fish
fillets, such as swordfish, monkfish
or gemfish
500 g (1 lb 2 oz) small squid tubes
12 mussels
12 clams (vongole)
12 raw prawns (shrimp)
3 large flat-leaf (Italian) parsley sprigs

ROMESCO SAUCE
80 g (23/4 oz/1/2 cup) blanched almonds
285 g (10 oz) jar roasted red capsicums
(peppers), drained and rinsed
2 teaspoons sweet paprika
2 slices stale white bread, torn into
large pieces
2 garlic cloves, roughly chopped
2 tablespoons sherry vinegar
125 ml (4 fl oz/1/2 cup) extra virgin olive oil

SERVES 6

Combine the wine, saffron, garlic, leek, red and green capsicum, paprika, tomatoes, almonds, bay leaf, chilli, brandy, lemon juice and stock in the slow cooker. Cook on high for 3 hours.

Meanwhile, prepare the seafood. Cut the fish into 2 cm (3/4 inch) cubes. Clean the squid tubes and cut into rings. Scrub the mussels and clams with a stiff brush. Pull out the hairy beards from the mussels. Discard any broken mussels or clams or open ones that don't close when tapped on the work surface. Peel the prawns, leaving the tails intact. Gently pull out the dark vein from each prawn back, starting at the head end.

Add the prepared seafood and parsley to the slow cooker and cook for a further 30 minutes, or until the seafood is cooked and the mussels and clams have opened. Discard any that remain closed. Remove the parsley from the soup.

To make the romesco sauce, place the almonds, roasted capsicum, paprika, bread pieces, garlic and vinegar in the bowl of a food processor. Process until smooth, then gradually add enough of the olive oil until you have a thick sauce.

Stir enough of the romesco sauce through the zarzuela to thicken it slightly. Divide among serving bowls and top with the remaining sauce. Serve with crusty bread.

PREPARATION TIME: 40 MINUTES   COOKING TIME: 3 1/2 HOURS

May 1/11
Chicken tender & tasty, but skin not browned at all.
Dressing delicious & garlicky!

CHICKEN COOKED IN WHITE WINE

40 g (1½ oz/½ cup) fresh breadcrumbs
4 garlic cloves, crushed
3 rosemary sprigs, leaves removed and chopped
1 teaspoon grated lemon zest
1.5 kg (3 lb 5 oz) chicken
200 ml (7 fl oz) chicken stock
200 ml (7 fl oz) white wine

SERVES 4

In a small bowl, combine the breadcrumbs, garlic, rosemary and lemon zest to make the stuffing.

Rinse the chicken inside and out and pat dry with paper towel. Loosely stuff the body cavity of the chicken with the stuffing, then tie or skewer the legs together to secure the stuffing inside the chicken.

Put the stock and wine in a small saucepan and bring to the boil. Remove from the heat.

Put the chicken, breast side down, in the slow cooker and pour over the stock and wine mixture. Cook on low for 6 hours, or until the chicken is tender and the juices run clear when the thigh is pierced with a skewer. Carve the chicken into pieces and serve with steamed buttered potatoes and green vegetables if desired.

PREPARATION TIME: 40 MINUTES   COOKING TIME: 6 HOURS

HOWTOWDIE

STUFFING
85 g (3 oz/²/₃ cup) oatmeal
2 tablespoons shredded suet or dripping
(see Notes)
1 small onion, finely chopped
1¹/₂ tablespoons chopped flat-leaf
(Italian) parsley
¹/₂ teaspoon finely grated lemon zest
1¹/₂ tablespoons whisky

1.8 kg (4 lb) chicken
1 leek, white part only, sliced
1 bay leaf
very small pinch ground cloves
pinch freshly grated nutmeg
500 ml (17 fl oz/2 cups) chicken stock
1–2 chicken livers, chopped
60 ml (2 fl oz/¹/₄ cup) thick
(double/heavy) cream

SERVES 4–6

To make the stuffing, toast the oatmeal in a frying pan over medium heat until golden and aromatic. Remove to a bowl. Add the suet to the pan and, when it is bubbling, add the onion and cook for 5 minutes, or until soft and lightly golden. Add to the bowl with the oatmeal along with the parsley, lemon zest and whisky. Stir to combine so that the mixture is loosely bound. If it is too dry, add 1 tablespoon water or chicken stock. Season well with salt and freshly ground black pepper and allow to cool completely before stuffing the chicken.

Rinse the chicken inside and out and allow to dry. Loosely fill the chicken with the stuffing, then tie or skewer the legs together to secure the stuffing inside the chicken. Put the chicken in the slow cooker along with the leek, bay leaf, cloves, nutmeg and stock. Cook on low for 4 hours, or until the chicken is tender and the juices run clear when the thigh is pierced with a skewer.

Carefully lift the chicken out of the slow cooker, transfer it to a plate and cover to keep warm while you finish the sauce.

Purée the chicken livers in the small bowl of a food processor. Remove all but 250 ml (9 fl oz/1 cup) of liquid from the slow cooker. Add the puréed chicken livers to the liquid left in the slow cooker and stir until they melt into the sauce. Add the cream and cook for a few minutes, or until the sauce is heated through, but don't allow it to boil. (For a smoother sauce, strain the cooking liquid before adding the livers and cream.)

Serve the chicken whole or carved with the sauce poured over and a little of the stuffing on the side. Serve with green vegetables such as blanched green beans and wilted spinach.

PREPARATION TIME: 30 MINUTES   COOKING TIME: 4¹/₄ HOURS

NOTES: Howtowdie is a traditional Scottish recipe of roast chicken with oat stuffing.
    Suet is a firm, white fat available from most butchers.

CHICKEN AGRODOLCE

1.2 kg (2 lb 10 oz) chicken pieces, skin removed
1 garlic clove
1 tablespoon dried oregano
2 bay leaves
125 ml (4 fl oz/^{1}/$_2$ cup) red wine vinegar
125 ml (4 fl oz/^{1}/$_2$ cup) dry white wine
55 g (2 oz/^{1}/$_4$ cup firmly packed) soft brown sugar
220 g (7^3/$_4$ oz/1 cup) pitted prunes
2 tablespoons capers, rinsed
175 g (6 oz/1 cup) green olives
1 handful flat-leaf (Italian) parsley, chopped

SERVES 6

Combine the chicken, garlic, oregano, bay leaves, vinegar, wine and brown sugar in the slow cooker. Cook on low for 3 hours.

Stir in the prunes, capers and olives and cook for a further 30 minutes, or until the chicken is cooked through. Season with salt and freshly ground black pepper and stir through the parsley. Serve with mashed potato.

PREPARATION TIME: 30 MINUTES   COOKING TIME: 3^1/$_2$ HOURS

CHICKEN WITH CELERIAC AND MARJORAM

1 kg (2 lb 4 oz) boneless, skinless chicken thighs
1 leek, white part only, sliced
1 garlic clove, crushed
1 large celeriac, trimmed, peeled and diced
250 ml (9 fl oz/1 cup) chicken stock
2 small marjoram sprigs
300 ml (10^1/$_2$ fl oz) pouring cream
1 handful flat-leaf (Italian) parsley, chopped

SERVES 6

Trim the chicken thighs of any fat and cut them into quarters. Combine the chicken pieces, leek, garlic, celeriac, stock and marjoram in the slow cooker. Cook on high for 2^1/$_2$ hours. Add the cream and cook for a further 30 minutes.

Season to taste with salt and freshly ground black pepper. Stir through the parsley and serve with steamed asparagus if desired.

PREPARATION TIME: 10 MINUTES   COOKING TIME: 3 HOURS

COQ AU VIN

2 x 1.5 kg (3 lb 5 oz) chickens (see Note)
2 bay leaves
2 thyme sprigs
250 g (9 oz) bacon, diced
20 baby onions, peeled
375 ml (13 fl oz/1½ cups) red wine
1 litre (35 fl oz/4 cups) chicken stock
125 ml (4 fl oz/½ cup) brandy
2 teaspoons tomato paste
(concentrated purée)
250 g (9 oz) button mushrooms
60 g (2¼ oz) butter, softened
40 g (1½ oz/⅓ cup) plain (all-purpose)
flour

SERVES 8

Joint each chicken into eight pieces by removing both legs and cutting between the joint of the drumstick and the thigh. Cut down either side of the backbone and lift it out. Turn the chicken over and cut through the cartilage down the centre of the breastbone. Cut each breast in half, leaving the wing attached to the top half.

Put the chicken pieces, bay leaves, thyme, bacon, onions, wine, stock, brandy and tomato paste in the slow cooker. Cook on high for 3 hours, or until the chicken is almost cooked through.

Add the mushrooms and cook for a further 30 minutes. Lift out the chicken and vegetables and place them on a plate, cover and set aside.

Mix together the butter and flour and whisk into the sauce in the slow cooker. Cook on high for about 10 minutes, stirring, until thickened, then return the chicken and vegetables to the sauce to heat through. Serve with steamed potatoes.

PREPARATION TIME: 15 MINUTES   COOKING TIME: 3¾ HOURS

NOTE: Alternatively, buy 3 kg (6 lb 12 oz) chicken pieces.

Feb 10
Excellent served c̄ mashed potatoes or a couscous c̄ chopped mint +
toasted pecan bits + juice of ½ lemon
+ 1 tbsp olive oil

CHICKEN WITH TARRAGON AND FENNEL

300 g (10½ oz) kipfler (fingerling) potatoes
1 large fennel bulb *used celery + 2 carrots*
1 red onion
1.8 kg (4 lb) chicken
1 lemon
2–3 tablespoons extra virgin olive oil
4 garlic cloves, finely chopped
didn't use 3 tarragon sprigs
125 ml (4 fl oz/½ cup) chicken stock
used 1 can chicken stock undiluted 125 ml (4 fl oz/½ cup) verjuice
250 g (9 oz) cherry tomatoes
2 tablespoons chopped flat-leaf (Italian) parsley

1 bay leaf

SERVES 6

Peel the potatoes and cut into 2 cm (³/4 inch) pieces. Cover with water and set aside.

Remove the tough outer shell of the fennel. Slice into 8–10 wedges, leaving the root section attached so each fennel wedge doesn't fall apart. Peel the onion and cut it into 8–10 wedges, again using the root section to hold the wedges together.

Rinse the chicken inside and out and pat dry with paper towel. Cut the lemon in half and place in the chicken cavity. Sprinkle the chicken with salt and set aside.

Heat the oil in a heavy-based non-stick frying pan over medium heat. Add the fennel and onion wedges and cook, in batches if necessary, for about 5 minutes until golden brown. Add the garlic, reduce the heat to low and cook for about 2 minutes, or until lightly browned.

Drain the potatoes and put them in the slow cooker along with the fennel, onion and garlic. Top with the tarragon.

Return the frying pan to medium heat, add the whole chicken and cook, turning until browned all over, for about 3 minutes each side. Place the browned chicken on top of the vegetables in the slow cooker. Pour in the stock, verjuice and add the tomatoes. Cook on low for 6 hours, or until the chicken is cooked through and tender and the juices run clear when the thigh is pierced with a skewer.

Season to taste with salt and freshly ground black pepper and serve sprinkled with chopped parsley.

PREPARATION TIME: 25 MINUTES   COOKING TIME: 6¼ HOURS

SPANISH-STYLE DUCK WITH PEARS

2 kg (4 lb 8 oz) duck
$1/4$ teaspoon freshly grated nutmeg
$1/2$ teaspoon smoked paprika
pinch ground cloves
2 firm ripe pears, peeled, quartered and cored
8 French shallots, peeled
8 baby carrots, trimmed
2 garlic cloves, sliced
1 bay leaf
1 thyme sprig
1 cinnamon stick
80 ml ($2^1/2$ fl oz/$1/3$ cup) sherry
750 ml (26 fl oz/3 cups) chicken stock
100 g ($3^1/2$ oz/$2/3$ cup) whole almonds, toasted
25 g (1 oz) dark bittersweet chocolate, roughly chopped

SERVES 4

Trim the duck of excess fat and then joint it into eight pieces.

In a small bowl, mix together the nutmeg, paprika, cloves and a little salt and freshly ground black pepper. Dust the duck pieces with the spice mixture.

Put the duck in the slow cooker along with the pears, shallots and carrots. Add the garlic, bay leaf, thyme, cinnamon stick, sherry and stock. Cook on low for 5 hours, or until the duck is tender and cooked. Skim the surface of any fat.

Meanwhile, finely grind the almonds and chocolate in a food processor. Transfer to a bowl.

When the duck is cooked, lift the duck, pears, shallots, carrots and cinnamon stick out of the liquid using a slotted spoon and transfer to a serving dish. Cover and keep warm.

Simmer the liquid left in the slow cooker, uncovered, for 10 minutes. Remove 250 ml (9 fl oz/1 cup) of the hot liquid and stir into the ground almonds and chocolate. Whisk the chocolate mixture back into the liquid in the slow cooker until the sauce has thickened. Season to taste, then pour the sauce over the duck and serve.

PREPARATION TIME: 30 MINUTES   COOKING TIME: $5^1/4$ HOURS

RABBIT WITH MUSTARD

60 g (2¼ oz/½ cup) plain (all-purpose)
flour
2 kg (4 lb 8 oz) farmed rabbit, jointed
1 tablespoon olive oil
20 g (¾ oz) butter
200 g (7 oz) bacon, finely chopped
250 ml (9 fl oz/1 cup) white wine
1 onion, finely chopped
2 carrots, finely chopped
1 garlic clove, crushed
250 ml (9 fl oz/1 cup) chicken stock
3 tablespoons dijon mustard
2 bay leaves
300 ml (10½ fl oz) pouring cream
flat-leaf (Italian) parsley, to garnish

SERVES 6–8

Put the flour in a shallow dish and season well with salt and freshly ground black pepper. Coat the rabbit pieces in a dusting of the seasoned flour. Heat the oil and butter in a large frying pan over medium heat and cook the rabbit pieces for 3–4 minutes each side, or until golden. Transfer to the slow cooker.

Add the bacon to the frying pan and cook for 5 minutes, or until crisp. Add to the slow cooker. Pour off any fat from the pan and deglaze with the wine, stirring well. Pour the wine into the slow cooker.

Add the onion, carrot, garlic, stock, half of the mustard, the bay leaves and cream to the slow cooker. Cook on low for 3 hours, or until the rabbit is tender and cooked through.

Stir in the remaining mustard and season to taste with salt and freshly ground black pepper. Before serving, sprinkle with parsley and serve with boiled potatoes.

PREPARATION TIME: 20 MINUTES   COOKING TIME: 3¼ HOURS

BRAISED PORK NECK WITH ORANGE AND STAR ANISE

1 large handful flat-leaf (Italian) parsley
1 tablespoon ground cinnamon
1 tablespoon grated fresh ginger
2 garlic cloves, crushed
1.6 kg (3 lb 8 oz) pork neck (pork scotch) fillet
1 orange, peeled and segmented
80 ml (2^1/$_2$ fl oz/^{1}/$_3$ cup) olive oil
4 star anise

SERVES 6

Put the parsley in a heatproof bowl and pour over enough boiling water to cover. Strain, then transfer the blanched parsley to the small bowl of a food processor along with the cinnamon, ginger and garlic. Process to a paste.

Slice the pork lengthways along the middle and open it out flat on a clean work surface. Brush with the parsley and cinnamon paste and lay orange segments along the centre. Roll the pork tightly to form a cylinder, enclosing the orange, and tie at intervals with kitchen string. Brush the pork with the olive oil and generously season with sea salt and freshly ground black pepper.

Heat the remaining oil in a large frying pan and seal the pork on high for 4 minutes on each side, or until golden all over.

Put the pork in the slow cooker along with the star anise and cook on high for 4 hours, or until the pork is tender and cooked through. Season with salt and freshly ground black pepper. Serve the pork with mashed sweet potato.

PREPARATION TIME: 30 MINUTES   COOKING TIME: 4^1/$_4$ HOURS

PORK COOKED IN MILK

2 kg (4 lb 8 oz) pork loin rack,
with 6 chops
6 baby potatoes, peeled and halved
1 large fennel bulb, cut into thick wedges
2 garlic cloves, halved lengthways
2 rosemary sprigs
1 litre (35 fl oz/4 cups) milk
grated zest of 2 lemons
juice of 1 lemon

SERVES 6

Trim the pork of most of the excess fat. Put the pork, potato, fennel, garlic, rosemary, milk, lemon zest and lemon juice in the slow cooker. Cook on low for 6 hours, or until the pork is tender.

Transfer the pork and vegetables to a serving platter. Cover with foil and set aside to rest for 10 minutes. While the pork is resting, increase the slow cooker heat to high and reduce the liquid left in the bowl. Taste and check for seasoning.

Strain the sauce if you like (you don't need to, but it may look curdled) and serve with the pork and vegetables.

PREPARATION TIME: 15 MINUTES   COOKING TIME: 6^1/4 HOURS

PORK LOIN RACK WITH PANCETTA AND SWEET POTATO

1.2 kg (2 lb 10 oz) pork loin rack,
with 4 chops
90 g (3^1/4 oz) piece pancetta,
1 cm (1/2 inch) thick, diced
6 bulb spring onions (scallions), trimmed
with 3 cm (1^1/4 inch) stem,
halved lengthways
2 garlic cloves, chopped
350 g (12 oz) purple-skinned sweet potato,
chopped into 5 cm (2 inch) chunks
250 ml (9 fl oz/1 cup) sparkling apple
juice (cider)
1 cinnamon stick
1 tablespoon cornflour (cornstarch)
2 tablespoons chopped flat-leaf (Italian)
parsley

SERVES 4

Trim the pork of skin and fat and press some sea salt and freshly ground black pepper over the pork.

Put the pork, diced pancetta, spring onions, garlic, sweet potato, apple juice and cinnamon stick in the slow cooker. Cook on high for 4-5 hours, or until the pork is tender. Transfer the pork and vegetables to a serving platter. Cover with foil and allow to rest. Remove the cinnamon stick.

While the pork is resting, combine the cornflour with a little water to make a smooth paste and stir into the juices in the slow cooker. Cook for a further 5-10 minutes to thicken the juices a little.

To serve, cut through the loin to serve a chop per person. Spoon over the vegetables and some juices. Scatter over the parsley.

PREPARATION TIME: 20 MINUTES   COOKING TIME: 4-5 HOURS

BRAISED PORK LOIN WITH CABBAGE AND POTATO

2 teaspoons fennel seeds

2 teaspoons caraway seeds

1 teaspoon sea salt

$^1/_2$ teaspoon paprika

1.2 kg (2 lb 10 oz) boned, rolled pork loin

1 tablespoon olive oil

1 bacon slice, cut into small dice

1 small onion, thinly sliced

1 tablespoon dijon mustard

60 ml (2 fl oz/$^1/_4$ cup) white wine

60 ml (2 fl oz/$^1/_4$ cup) chicken stock

1 tablespoon vinegar

125 ml (4 fl oz/$^1/_2$ cup) pouring cream

3 all-purpose potatoes, peeled

$^1/_2$ small red cabbage, finely shredded

SERVES 6

Using a mortar and pestle or spice grinder, crush the fennel seeds, caraway seeds, sea salt and paprika. Push three-quarters of the spice mixture inside the rolled pork, through the gaps at either end. Sprinkle the remaining spice mixture over the pork.

Heat the olive oil in a non-stick frying pan over medium heat. Add the pork and brown on all sides (about 1 minute per side), and set aside. Add the bacon and onion to the pan and sauté for 3 minutes, or until softened. Add the mustard, wine, stock, vinegar and cream and stir to combine. Remove the pan from the heat.

Thinly slice the potatoes using either a very sharp knife or a mandolin. Layer the potatoes in the base of the slow cooker and sprinkle each layer with salt. Next add the cabbage, top with the bacon and cream mixture, then add the pork. Cook on low for 4 hours, or until the pork is very tender.

Remove the pork to a board and slice. Serve the pork with the potato and cabbage and top with the sauce.

PREPARATION TIME: 30 MINUTES   COOKING TIME: 4$^1/_4$ HOURS

VEAL OLIVES WITH PROSCIUTTO, CHEESE AND SAGE

TOMATO AND OLIVE SAUCE
400 g (14 oz) tinned chopped tomatoes
2 semi-dried (sun-blushed) tomatoes, chopped
2 spring onions (scallions), chopped
2 garlic cloves, crushed
10 black olives, pitted and chopped
1 teaspoon caster (superfine) sugar

6 x 150 g (5¹/₂ oz) veal leg steaks (schnitzel)
6 prosciutto slices, trimmed of fat
50 g (1³/₄ oz/¹/₂ cup) freshly grated parmesan cheese
finely grated zest of 1 lemon
12 sage leaves
1 tablespoon olive oil
20 g (³/₄ oz) butter
1 tablespoon cornflour (cornstarch) (optional)
extra sage leaves, to garnish

SERVES 4

To make the tomato and olive sauce, combine the tomatoes, semi-dried tomatoes, spring onion, garlic, olives and sugar in a bowl. Season with salt and freshly ground black pepper. Pour half the tomato sauce into the slow cooker and set the remainder aside.

Put each veal steak between two sheets of plastic wrap and use the flat side of a meat mallet to pound them to about 5 mm (¹/₄ inch) thick and roughly 25 x 10 cm (10 x 4 inches) in size.

Lay the prosciutto slices along the top of each veal steak. Evenly divide the parmesan, lemon zest and sage leaves along each piece of veal. Season with freshly ground black pepper. Roll up the veal and secure with a toothpick to form veal olives.

Heat the oil and butter in a large frying pan. When the oil is hot, add the veal olives and cook for 5 minutes, turning frequently until browned. Arrange the veal olives over the tomato sauce in the slow cooker. They will be packed in side by side. Pour over the remaining tomato sauce. Cook on low for 6–8 hours, or until the veal is tender. Remove the veal olives to a side plate and remove the toothpicks, cover and keep warm.

If you like, you can thicken the sauce. Combine the cornflour in a bowl with 1 tablespoon water until smooth, then stir into the sauce. Stir over high heat until thickened.

To serve, cut each veal olive into three or four thick slices diagonally and arrange onto serving plates. Pour over the sauce and garnish with an extra sage leaf or two. Serve with mashed potato or polenta and a green vegetable or salad.

PREPARATION TIME: 30 MINUTES   COOKING TIME: 6–8 HOURS

VEAL BRAISED WITH LEMON THYME

2 tablespoons olive oil
1.5 kg (3 lb 5 oz) rack of veal (6 cutlets), trimmed to a neat shape
2 leeks, white part only, thinly sliced
30 g (1 oz) butter
1 tablespoon plain (all-purpose) flour
1 tablespoon grated lemon zest
125 ml (4 fl oz/^{1}/$_2$ cup) chicken stock
125 ml (4 fl oz/^{1}/$_2$ cup) white wine
2 tablespoons lemon thyme
125 ml (4 fl oz/^{1}/$_2$ cup) pouring cream

SERVES 4

Heat the oil in a deep heavy-based frying pan over medium heat and brown the veal well on all sides. Remove the veal from the pan and put in the slow cooker.

Add the leek and butter to the frying pan, reduce the heat and cook, stirring occasionally, for 10 minutes, or until soft. Add the flour to the pan and cook for 2 minutes, stirring continuously. Add the lemon zest and season with freshly ground black pepper. Stir in the stock and wine and bring to the boil, stirring continuously.

Add the leek mixture to the slow cooker. Cook on low for 3 hours, or until the veal is tender and cooked through.

Remove the veal to a plate, cover and set aside. Increase the slow cooker heat to high. Add the lemon thyme and cream and cook, uncovered, for a further 10 minutes. Season to taste with salt and freshly ground black pepper. Serve the veal with the sauce and with boiled baby potatoes.

PREPARATION TIME: 15 MINUTES   COOKING TIME: 3^1/$_2$ HOURS

VEAL WITH PEPERONATA AND GNOCCHI

PEPERONATA
400 g (14 oz) tinned whole tomatoes
1 red onion, cut into thin wedges
2 garlic cloves, chopped
1 red or green chilli, seeded and finely chopped (optional)
1 red capsicum (pepper), seeded and thinly sliced
1 yellow capsicum (pepper), seeded and thinly sliced
1 tablespoon red wine vinegar
1 teaspoon caster (superfine) sugar

60 g (2¹/₄ oz/¹/₂ cup) plain (all-purpose) flour
4 even-sized pieces (about 750 g/ 1 lb 10 oz) veal osso bucco (see Note)
20 g (³/₄ oz) butter
1 tablespoon olive oil
125 ml (4 fl oz/¹/₂ cup) white wine
350 g (12 oz) packet potato gnocchi

GREMOLATA
grated zest of 1 lemon
1 garlic clove, finely chopped
1 large handful flat-leaf (Italian) parsley, finely chopped

SERVES 4

To make the peperonata, put the tomatoes in a large bowl and roughly chop with scissors or a knife. Add the remaining peperonata ingredients and mix to combine. Season with salt and freshly ground black pepper. Add half of the peperonata to the slow cooker.

Put the flour in a flat dish and season well with salt and freshly ground black pepper. Trim the osso bucco pieces of excess fat and then coat the veal in the seasoned flour.

Heat the butter and oil in a large frying pan over medium heat. When the oil is hot, add the osso bucco and brown well for 2–3 minutes on each side. Pour in the wine and let it bubble and reduce a little. Arrange the browned veal in a single layer on top of the peperonata in the slow cooker. Pour in any juices left in the frying pan, then spoon over the remaining peperonata.

Cook on high for 4–6 hours, or until the veal is very tender. Remove the osso bucco to a side plate, cover and keep warm. Add the gnocchi to the peperonata in the slow cooker and stir to combine. Cover and cook for a further 20 minutes, or until the gnocchi is tender.

To make the gremolata, combine the lemon zest, garlic and parsley in a small bowl.

To serve, spoon the gnocchi and peperonata onto serving plates, top with the osso bucco and sprinkle over the gremolata.

PREPARATION TIME: 30 MINUTES   COOKING TIME: 4–6 HOURS

NOTE: Use veal chops instead of veal osso bucco if you prefer.

BRAISED VEAL SHANKS

4-6 veal shanks (about 2 kg/4 lb 8 oz)
200 g (7 oz/1²/₃ cups) plain
(all-purpose) flour
1 leek, white part only, finely diced
1 onion, finely diced
1 carrot, finely diced
1 celery stalk, finely diced
2 garlic cloves, finely chopped
1 bay leaf
1 rosemary sprig, leaves chopped
125 ml (4 fl oz/¹/₂ cup) red wine
500 ml (17 fl oz/2 cups) veal stock
200 g (7 oz) artichoke halves
80 g (2³/₄ oz/¹/₂ cup) frozen peas

ORANGE GREMOLATA
1 garlic clove, finely chopped
grated zest of 1 orange
1 small handful flat-leaf (Italian) parsley,
finely chopped

SERVES 4–6

Coat the veal shanks in the flour and shake off the excess. Put the veal in the slow cooker along with the leek, onion, carrot, celery, garlic, bay leaf, rosemary, wine and stock. Cook on high for 3 hours.

Add the artichokes to the slow cooker. Continue to cook on high, with the lid off, for 1 hour. Add the peas and cook for a further 5 minutes, or until the peas are cooked through. Season to taste with salt and freshly ground black pepper.

To make the orange gremolata, combine the garlic, orange zest and parsley. Serve the veal shanks sprinkled with the gremolata.

PREPARATION TIME: 30 MINUTES   COOKING TIME: 4 HOURS

VEAL, LEMON AND CAPER CASSEROLE

300 g (10¹/₂ oz) French shallots, unpeeled
1 kg (2 lb 4 oz) boneless veal shoulder
2 garlic cloves, crushed
3 leeks, white part only, cut into large chunks
2 tablespoons plain (all-purpose) flour
500 ml (17 fl oz/2 cups) chicken stock
1 teaspoon grated lemon zest
80 ml (2¹/₂ fl oz/¹/₃ cup) lemon juice
2 bay leaves
2 tablespoons capers, rinsed well
chopped flat-leaf (Italian) parsley, to serve
caperberries, to garnish (optional)

SERVES 4

Put the shallots in a heatproof bowl. Pour over boiling water to cover and set aside for 5 minutes to soften. Drain and peel.

Trim the veal and cut into 4 cm (1¹/₂ inch) cubes. Put the shallots and veal cubes in the slow cooker along with the garlic, leek, flour, stock, lemon zest, lemon juice and bay leaves. Stir to combine the ingredients. Cook on high for 4 hours, or until the veal is tender. During the last 30 minutes of cooking, remove the lid to allow the sauce to reduce a little.

To serve, stir in the capers and season with salt and freshly ground black pepper. Sprinkle with parsley and garnish with caperberries if desired.

PREPARATION TIME: 25 MINUTES   COOKING TIME: 4 HOURS

OXTAIL WITH MARMALADE

1.5 kg (3 lb 5 oz) oxtail
160 g (5^1/$_2$ oz/^{1}/$_2$ cup) marmalade
100 ml (3^1/$_2$ fl oz) sherry
2 tablespoons olive oil
4 all-purpose potatoes, cut into
3 cm (1^1/$_4$ inch) pieces
2 carrots, sliced
1 onion, thinly sliced
2 bay leaves
1 cinnamon stick
1 orange, peeled and segmented

SERVES 4

Cut the oxtail into sections, then combine with the marmalade and sherry in a large bowl. Cover and marinate overnight.

Heat the olive oil in a large frying pan over high heat and cook the oxtail in batches for about 4 minutes on each side, or until golden brown all over. Set aside.

Put the potato, carrot, onion, bay leaves and cinnamon stick in the slow cooker and sit the oxtail on top. Cook on high for 4 hours, or until the meat is tender. Season with salt and freshly ground black pepper. Top the oxtail with the orange segments and serve with mashed potato.

PREPARATION TIME: 20 MINUTES +   COOKING TIME: 4^1/$_4$ HOURS

BRAISED BEEF WITH TURNIPS AND HERBS

1 kg (2 lb 4 oz) chuck steak
150 g (5^1/$_2$ oz) bacon slices, diced
2 onions, thinly sliced
2 large turnips, halved, each half cut
into 4 wedges
125 ml (4 fl oz/^{1}/$_2$ cup) red wine
250 ml (9 fl oz/1 cup) beef stock
1^1/$_2$ tablespoons red wine vinegar
1 large mint sprig
1 small handful flat-leaf (Italian) parsley, chopped

SERVES 4–6

Trim the beef and cut into 4 cm (1^1/$_2$ inch) cubes. Combine the beef, bacon, onion, turnips, wine, stock, vinegar and mint in the slow cooker. Cook on low for 4 hours.

Season with salt and freshly ground black pepper. Remove the mint and stir through the parsley. Serve with mashed potato or bread.

PREPARATION TIME: 20 MINUTES   COOKING TIME: 4 HOURS

Oxtail with marmalade

PROSCIUTTO WRAPPED BEEF WITH BROAD BEANS

500 g (1 lb 2 oz) thick beef fillet
3 garlic cloves, thinly sliced
2 tablespoons chopped rosemary
8–10 thin slices prosciutto, pancetta or smoked bacon
2 tablespoons olive oil
20 g (³/₄ oz) dried wild mushrooms, such as porcini
1 onion, halved and sliced
170 ml (5¹/₂ fl oz) red wine
400 g (14 oz) tinned chopped tomatoes
400 g (14 oz) peeled broad (fava) beans

SERVES 4

Trim the beef of excess fat and make several small incisions around the beef. Push a slice of garlic into each incision, using up one of the garlic cloves. Sprinkle 1 tablespoon of the rosemary over the beef and season with salt and freshly ground black pepper.

Lay the prosciutto slices on a board in a line next to each other, creating a sheet of prosciutto to wrap the beef in. Place the beef fillet across them and fold the prosciutto over to enclose the beef. Tie several times with kitchen string to keep the beef and prosciutto together. Leave in the refrigerator to rest for at least 15 minutes.

Heat the olive oil in a large frying pan over high heat. Add the beef and sear on all sides until the prosciutto is golden brown, but not burnt. A little of the prosciutto might fall off, but it doesn't matter: just make sure the beef is well sealed. Remove from the pan.

Put the dried mushrooms in a bowl with 185 ml (6 fl oz/³/₄ cup) hot water and soak for 10 minutes.

Put the beef in the slow cooker along with the onion, remaining garlic and rosemary, the mushrooms and the soaking liquid, wine and tomatoes. Cook on low for 2 hours, or until the beef is tender.

Add the broad beans and cook for a further 20 minutes. Season with salt and freshly ground black pepper and serve with mashed potato or soft polenta.

PREPARATION TIME: 25 MINUTES +   COOKING TIME: 2¹/₂ HOURS

BEEF STROGANOFF WITH MIXED MUSHROOMS

325 g (11^1/$_2$ oz) new potatoes, unpeeled, cut into 1.5 cm (^{5}/8 inch) thick slices

300 g (10^1/$_2$ oz) mixed mushrooms, such as oyster and Swiss brown, thickly sliced

1 onion, thinly sliced into rings

2-3 garlic cloves, chopped

1 teaspoon dried oregano

750 g (1 lb 10 oz) round or sirloin steak

30 g (1 oz/^{1}/$_4$ cup) plain (all-purpose) flour

^{1}/$_2$ teaspoon paprika

2 tablespoons olive oil

125 ml (4 fl oz/^{1}/$_2$ cup) beef stock

125 ml (4 fl oz/^{1}/$_2$ cup) white wine

2 tablespoons tomato paste (concentrated purée)

125 g (4^1/$_2$ oz/^{1}/$_2$ cup) sour cream

1 small handful chopped flat-leaf (Italian) parsley

SERVES 4

Layer the sliced potatoes in the base of the slow cooker.

Put the mushrooms and onion in a large bowl. Sprinkle over the garlic and oregano and season well with salt and freshly ground black pepper.

Trim the beef of any fat, then cut it into thin strips across the grain. Pat dry with paper towel. Combine the flour and paprika in a flat dish.

Heat 2 teaspoons of the olive oil in a large frying pan over high heat. Working with a quarter of the meat at a time, dust the meat in the flour, shake off the excess, then add to the pan and toss for 1-2 minutes, or until the meat is browned all over. Transfer to the mushroom and onion mixture. Repeat with the remaining oil, beef and flour.

Add any remaining flour to the frying pan, then pour in the stock, wine and tomato paste and whisk together until hot. Pour over the meat mixture in the bowl and toss well to combine. Transfer to the slow cooker over the sliced potatoes. Cook on high for 3-4 hours, or until the beef is tender and the potatoes are cooked.

Just before serving, stir through the sour cream and half the parsley. Spoon onto serving plates and serve with the potatoes. Sprinkle with the remaining parsley.

PREPARATION TIME: 40 MINUTES   COOKING TIME: 3-4 HOURS

BEEF OSSO BUCCO

60 g (2¼ oz/½ cup) plain (all-purpose) flour
1 kg (2 lb 4 oz) beef osso bucco
2–3 tablespoons vegetable oil
1 onion, finely chopped
1 carrot, finely chopped
2 bay leaves
½ teaspoon black peppercorns
400 g (14 oz) tinned chopped tomatoes
185 ml (6 fl oz/¾ cup) white wine
155 g (5½ oz/1 cup) frozen peas
1 handful flat-leaf (Italian) parsley, chopped

GREMOLATA
2 garlic cloves, finely chopped
1 handful flat-leaf (Italian) parsley, chopped
grated zest of 2 lemons

SERVES 4

Put the flour in a flat dish and season with salt and freshly ground black pepper. Dust the osso bucco in the seasoned flour.

Heat the oil in a large frying pan over medium heat, add the osso bucco in batches and cook for about 5 minutes on each side, or until golden brown all over.

Put the onion, carrot, bay leaves, peppercorns and osso bucco in the slow cooker and pour over the tomatoes and wine. Cook on high for 5–6 hours, or until the beef is tender. Add the peas and cook for a further 5 minutes.

Just before the osso bucco is cooked, make the gremolata. Combine the garlic, parsley and lemon zest in a bowl, cover and set aside.

Before serving, season the beef with salt and freshly ground black pepper and stir through the parsley. Transfer to serving plates, sprinkle with gremolata and serve with mashed potatoes and steamed vegetables.

PREPARATION TIME: 30 MINUTES   COOKING TIME: 5–6 HOURS

PORTUGUESE BEEF

1.25 kg (2 lb 12 oz) chuck steak

2 garlic cloves, thinly sliced

175 g (6 oz) smoked bacon slices, chopped

250 ml (9 fl oz/1 cup) red wine

250 ml (9 fl oz/1 cup) beef stock

1 tablespoon sweet paprika

³/4 teaspoon smoked paprika

2 bay leaves

2 teaspoons dried oregano

20 g (³/4 oz) butter, at room temperature

2 tablespoons plain (all-purpose) flour

175 g (6 oz/1 cup) green olives

30 g (1 oz/¹/4 cup) slivered almonds

SERVES 6

Trim the beef and cut into 4 cm (1¹/2 inch) cubes. Put the beef, garlic, bacon, wine, stock, sweet paprika, smoked paprika, bay leaves and oregano in the slow cooker. Cook on low for 5 hours, or until the beef is tender.

Mix together the butter and flour. Add gradually to the beef in the slow cooker, stirring. Cook, uncovered, for a further 10 minutes, or until the mixture has thickened.

Stir through the olives and almonds and season with salt and freshly ground black pepper. Serve with mashed potato or steamed rice.

PREPARATION TIME: 20 MINUTES   COOKING TIME: 5¹/4 HOURS

BEEF WITH ROOT VEGETABLES AND BROAD BEANS

1.2 kg (2 lb 10 oz) chuck steak

¹/2 teaspoon dried thyme

1 leek, white part only, cut into 1 cm (¹/2 inch) thick slices

1 celery stalk, sliced

2 garlic cloves, chopped

2 parsnips, quartered

300 g (10¹/2 oz) orange sweet potato, cut into 8 wedges

1 swede (rutabaga), cut into 8 wedges

250 ml (9 fl oz/1 cup) red wine

60 ml (2 fl oz/¹/4 cup) tomato sauce (ketchup)

1 tablespoon cornflour (cornstarch)

175 g (6 oz) frozen broad (fava) beans

SERVES 4

Trim the beef and cut into 4 cm (1¹/2 inch) cubes. Put the beef in the slow cooker, sprinkle over the thyme and season well with salt and freshly ground black pepper. Add the leek, celery, garlic, parsnip, sweet potato, swede, wine and tomato sauce. Cook on high for 4 hours, or until the beef is tender.

About 20 minutes before the end of cooking, combine the cornflour with a little water to make a smooth paste and stir into the beef and vegetables along with the broad beans. Continue to cook until the broad beans are cooked through, then serve.

PREPARATION TIME: 20 MINUTES   COOKING TIME: 4 HOURS

Portuguese beef

BEEF CHEEKS WITH ONIONS, MUSHROOMS AND THYME

1 kg (2 lb 4 oz) beef cheeks

100 g (3^1/$_2$ oz) bacon or speck, trimmed of fat, chopped

250 ml (9 fl oz/1 cup) red wine

2 celery stalks, finely chopped

1 carrot, finely chopped

1 onion, finely chopped

10 g (^{1}/$_4$ oz) thyme

3 garlic cloves

250 ml (9 fl oz/1 cup) beef stock

40 g (1^1/$_2$ oz) butter

12 baby onions, peeled and trimmed, halved lengthways if large

1^1/$_2$ tablespoons sugar

1^1/$_2$ tablespoons sherry vinegar

16 button mushrooms, halved

SERVES 4

Trim the beef cheeks of excess fat and sinew, then cut into four portions. Put the beef in the slow cooker along with the bacon, wine, celery, carrot, onion, thyme, garlic and stock. Cook on low for 7 hours (this will vary slightly, depending on the thickness of the beef), or until the meat is almost falling apart.

Meanwhile, place half of the butter in a heavy-based frying pan, add the onions and cook over low–medium heat for about 8 minutes, or until golden. Add the sugar and cook until caramelised, shaking the pan occasionally to ensure that it caramelises evenly. Add half the vinegar and stir to remove any sediment from the bottom of the pan. Transfer to the slow cooker.

Melt the remaining butter in the pan and cook the mushrooms over medium heat for 5–6 minutes, or until golden. Pour in the remaining vinegar and stir to remove any sediment from the bottom of the pan. Add the mushrooms to the slow cooker and cook, uncovered, for a further 1 hour, or until the beef is tender and the sauce has reduced and thickened slightly.

Serve the beef cheeks with the sauce, and with mashed potato and steamed green vegetables.

PREPARATION TIME: 25 MINUTES   COOKING TIME: 8^1/$_4$ HOURS

LAMB SHANKS IN RED WINE

1 onion, finely diced
1 leek, white part only, finely diced
1 carrot, finely diced
2 celery stalks, finely diced
1.4 kg (3 lb 2 oz) lamb shanks (4 shanks, about 300–350 g/10^1/$_2$–12 oz each)
3 garlic cloves, sliced
4 large rosemary sprigs
4 prosciutto slices
60 g (2^1/$_4$ oz/^{1}/$_4$ cup) tomato paste (concentrated purée)
500 ml (17 fl oz/2 cups) beef stock
250 ml (9 fl oz/1 cup) red wine
90 g (3^1/$_4$ oz/^{1}/$_2$ cup) black olives
1 small handful flat-leaf (Italian) parsley, finely chopped

SERVES 4

Place the diced vegetables in the base of the slow cooker.

Make three or four small incisions in the meaty part of the lamb shanks. Insert the garlic slices into the incisions. Put a rosemary sprig on each lamb shank and wrap it with a slice of prosciutto. Secure the prosciutto with a toothpick.

Add the lamb shanks to the diced vegetables in the slow cooker. Top with the tomato paste, stock and wine and season with salt and freshly ground black pepper. Cook on high for 4^1/$_2$ hours.

Add the olives and cook, uncovered, for a further 5 minutes, or until the olives are warmed through. Stir through the parsley and serve.

PREPARATION TIME: 20 MINUTES   COOKING TIME: 4^1/$_2$ HOURS

NAVARIN OF LAMB

1 kg (2 lb 4 oz) boneless lean lamb
shoulder
200 g (7 oz) baby turnips
8 bulb spring onions (scallions), trimmed
175 g (6 oz) small potatoes, peeled
(halved if large)
1 onion, chopped
1 garlic clove, crushed
125 ml (4 fl oz/^{1}/$_{2}$ cup) chicken stock
125 ml (4 fl oz/^{1}/$_{2}$ cup) red wine
2 tablespoons tomato paste
(concentrated purée)
1 large rosemary sprig
2 thyme sprigs
1 bay leaf
18 baby carrots
155 g (5^{1}/$_{2}$ oz/1 cup) fresh or frozen peas
1 tablespoon redcurrant jelly
1 handful flat-leaf (Italian) parsley,
chopped

SERVES 4

Trim the lamb of any excess fat and cut into 3 cm (1^{1}/$_{4}$ inch) cubes.
Put the lamb, turnips, spring onions, potatoes, onion, garlic, stock, wine,
tomato paste, rosemary, thyme and bay leaf in the slow cooker. Stir to
combine. Cook on high for 3 hours, or until the lamb is almost tender.

Trim the carrots, leaving a little bit of green stalk. Add the carrots to
the slow cooker and cook for a further 40 minutes, or until the carrots
are tender.

Stir through the peas, redcurrant jelly and parsley and cook for a further
5 minutes, or until the peas are tender. Season with salt and freshly
ground black pepper before serving.

PREPARATION TIME: 20 MINUTES   COOKING TIME: 3^{3}/$_{4}$ HOURS

SLOW-COOKED LAMB IN RED WINE

2 kg (4 lb 8 oz) lamb leg
50 g (1³/4 oz) butter, softened
2¹/2 tablespoons plain (all-purpose) flour

MARINADE
750 ml (26 fl oz) red wine, such as
burgundy or cabernet sauvignon
60 ml (2 fl oz/¹/4 cup) brandy
10 garlic cloves, bruised
1 tablespoon chopped rosemary
2 teaspoons chopped thyme
2 fresh bay leaves, torn into small pieces
1 large carrot, diced
1 large celery stalk, diced
1 onion, finely chopped
60 ml (2 fl oz/¹/4 cup) olive oil

SERVES 6

Trim any really thick pieces of fat from the lamb but leave it with a decent covering all over if possible.

Combine the marinade ingredients in a non-metallic baking dish, then add the lamb and turn to coat in the marinade. Cover and refrigerate for 24-48 hours, turning occasionally so the marinade is evenly distributed. Make sure you wrap and rewrap the dish tightly with plastic wrap each time to ensure the strong odours from the marinade do not permeate other foods in the refrigerator.

Put the lamb and marinade in the slow cooker. Cook on low for 10 hours, or until the lamb is tender and cooked.

Carefully remove the lamb to a serving platter using two wide spatulas. Cover the lamb with foil and a tea towel to keep warm while you make the sauce.

Drain off the fat from the liquid in the slow cooker. Transfer the ingredients left in the bowl of the slow cooker to a food processor. Purée, then strain the liquid back into the slow cooker. Turn the slow cooker heat to high. Mix together the softened butter and flour and gradually whisk it into the sauce. Continue cooking for a further 10–15 minutes, or until the sauce has thickened slightly.

Carve the lamb and serve with the sauce. Serve with green vegetables and potato gratin.

PREPARATION TIME: 20 MINUTES +   COOKING TIME: 10¹/4 HOURS

HOT AND SPICY

CHICKPEA AND VEGETABLE CURRY

3 garlic cloves, crushed

1 red or green chilli, seeded and chopped

2 tablespoons Indian curry paste

1 teaspoon ground cumin

$^1/_2$ teaspoon ground turmeric

400 g (14 oz) tinned chopped tomatoes

250 ml (9 fl oz/1 cup) vegetable stock or water

1 red onion, cut into thin wedges

1 large carrot, sliced diagonally into 3 cm (1$^1/_4$ inch) chunks

250 g (9 oz) orange sweet potato, sliced diagonally into 3 cm (1$^1/_4$ inch) chunks

250 g (9 oz) cauliflower, cut into florets

250 g (9 oz) broccoli, cut into florets

2 long, thin eggplants (aubergines), about 100 g (3$^1/_2$ oz) in total, cut into 3 cm (1$^1/_4$ inch) thick slices

400 g (14 oz) tinned chickpeas, drained and rinsed

155 g (5$^1/_2$ oz/1 cup) fresh or frozen peas

165 ml (5$^1/_2$ fl oz) tinned coconut milk

1 small handful coriander (cilantro) leaves, to garnish

SERVES 4–6

Combine the garlic, chilli, curry paste, cumin, turmeric, tomatoes and stock in the slow cooker. Stir in the onion, carrot, sweet potato, cauliflower, broccoli, eggplant and chickpeas. Cook on high for 3–4 hours, or until all the vegetables are cooked.

Add the peas and stir through the coconut milk. Continue to cook for a further 10 minutes, or until the peas are cooked through.

To serve, ladle the curry into large bowls and sprinkle with the coriander leaves. Serve with rice.

PREPARATION TIME: 30 MINUTES   COOKING TIME: 3–4 HOURS

NOTE: You can add a little more curry paste if you prefer a stronger curry flavour.

YELLOW CURRY WITH VEGETABLES

100 g (3¹/₂ oz) cauliflower
1 long, thin eggplant (aubergine)
1 small red capsicum (pepper)
2 small zucchini (courgettes)
150 g (5¹/₂ oz) green beans
1–2 tablespoons yellow curry paste
500 ml (17 fl oz/2 cups) coconut cream
125 ml (4 fl oz/¹/₂ cup) vegetable stock
150 g (5¹/₂ oz) baby corn
1¹/₂ tablespoons fish sauce
2 teaspoons grated palm sugar (jaggery) or soft brown sugar
1 small red chilli, seeded and chopped, to garnish
coriander (cilantro) leaves, to garnish

SERVES 4

Prepare the vegetables. Cut the cauliflower into florets and cut the eggplant, capsicum and zucchini into 1 cm (¹/₂ inch) slices. Cut the beans into 3 cm (1¹/₄ inch) lengths.

Put the cauliflower, eggplant and capsicum in the slow cooker with the curry paste, coconut cream and stock. Cook on low for 2 hours, or until the cauliflower is tender.

Stir in the zucchini, beans, corn, fish sauce and sugar and cook for a further 1 hour, or until the vegetables are tender. Garnish with the chilli and coriander and serve with steamed rice.

PREPARATION TIME: 30 MINUTES   COOKING TIME: 3 HOURS

DHAL

400 g (14 oz/2 cups) red lentils
1 onion, chopped
2 garlic cloves, chopped
2 teaspoons ground turmeric
2 teaspoons finely chopped fresh ginger
2 bay leaves
1 cinnamon stick
2 teaspoons ground cumin
1 teaspoon ground coriander
1 teaspoon mustard seeds
750 ml (26 fl oz/3 cups) chicken or vegetable stock
1 teaspoon garam masala
40 g (1¹/₂ oz) butter
2 large handfuls coriander (cilantro) leaves, chopped

SERVES 8

Put the lentils, onion, garlic, turmeric, ginger, bay leaves, cinnamon stick, cumin, ground coriander, mustard seeds, stock and 1 litre (35 fl oz/4 cups) water in the slow cooker. Cook on low for 4 hours, or until the lentils are soft.

Stir in the garam masala, butter and coriander leaves. Stir until the butter has melted, then serve.

PREPARATION TIME: 15 MINUTES   COOKING TIME: 4 HOURS

SPICY FISH CURRY

400 ml (14 fl oz) tinned coconut milk

5 green chillies, seeded and chopped

2 dried red chillies, chopped into pieces

1/2 cinnamon stick

2 teaspoons grated fresh ginger

2 garlic cloves, finely chopped

4 stalks fresh curry leaves (optional)

1 teaspoon ground turmeric

1/4 teaspoon chilli powder

1 teaspoon curry powder

2 tomatoes, finely chopped

250 ml (9 fl oz/1 cup) fish or chicken stock

800 g (1 lb 12 oz) snapper fillets, cubed

2 spring onions (scallions), sliced diagonally

juice of 2 limes, to taste

SERVES 4

Put the coconut milk, green and red chilli, cinnamon stick, ginger, garlic, curry leaves (if using), turmeric, chilli powder, curry powder, tomato and stock in the slow cooker. Cook on low for 2 hours, or until the flavours have developed.

Add the fish and cook for a further 30 minutes, or until the fish is cooked through and flakes when tested with a fork. Stir through half of the spring onion and add most of the lime juice, then taste to see if more lime juice is needed. Serve with rice and garnish with the remaining spring onion.

PREPARATION TIME: 20 MINUTES   COOKING TIME: 2 1/2 HOURS

CREAMY CHICKEN CURRY

2 cm (³/4 inch) piece fresh ginger, roughly chopped
3 garlic cloves, roughly chopped
1 kg (2 lb 4 oz) boneless, skinless chicken thighs
75 g (2¹/2 oz/¹/2 cup) blanched almonds
150 g (5¹/2 oz) Greek-style yoghurt
¹/2 teaspoon chilli powder
¹/4 teaspoon ground cloves
¹/4 teaspoon ground cinnamon
1 teaspoon garam masala
4 cardamom pods, lightly crushed
400 g (14 oz) tinned chopped tomatoes
1 large onion, thinly sliced
1 handful coriander (cilantro) leaves, finely chopped
80 ml (2¹/2 fl oz/¹/3 cup) thick (double/heavy) cream

SERVES 4

Using a mortar and pestle or a food processor, crush or blend the ginger and garlic together to form a paste. Alternatively, finely grate the ginger and crush the garlic and mix them together.

Trim the chicken of any excess fat and cut into fairly large pieces. Set aside while you prepare the marinade.

Grind the almonds in a food processor or finely chop them with a knife. Put the ginger and garlic paste and almonds in a large bowl with the yoghurt, chilli powder, cloves, cinnamon, garam masala, cardamom pods, tomatoes and 1 teaspoon salt. Blend together with a fork. Add the chicken pieces and stir to coat the chicken thoroughly. Cover and marinate for 2 hours, or overnight, in the refrigerator.

Combine the chicken mixture with the onion in the slow cooker. Cook on high for 3 hours. Add half the coriander and the cream and cook for a further 1 hour, or until the chicken is tender.

Season to taste with salt and freshly ground black pepper. Serve the chicken with rice and garnish with the remaining coriander.

PREPARATION TIME: 30 MINUTES +   COOKING TIME: 4 HOURS

CHICKEN BRAISED WITH GINGER AND STAR ANISE

1 kg (2 lb 4 oz) boneless, skinless chicken thighs
1 teaspoon sichuan peppercorns
3 x 2 cm (1^1/$_4$ x ^{3}/$_4$ inch) piece fresh ginger, shredded
2 garlic cloves, chopped
80 ml (2^1/$_2$ fl oz/^{1}/$_3$ cup) Chinese rice wine
60 ml (2 fl oz/^{1}/$_4$ cup) light soy sauce
1 tablespoon honey
1 star anise
3 spring onions (scallions), thinly sliced diagonally

SERVES 4

Trim the chicken of any fat, then cut each thigh in half. Put the chicken pieces, peppercorns, ginger, garlic, rice wine, soy sauce, honey and star anise in the slow cooker. Cook on high for 2 hours, or until the chicken is tender and cooked through.

Season with salt and freshly ground black pepper. Garnish with the spring onions and serve with steamed rice.

PREPARATION TIME: 15 MINUTES   COOKING TIME: 2 HOURS

GREEN CHICKEN CURRY

750 g (1 lb 10 oz) boneless, skinless chicken thighs
2 tablespoons green curry paste
435 ml (15^1/$_4$ fl oz/1^3/$_4$ cups) coconut milk
350 g (12 oz) long, thin eggplants (aubergines), sliced
7 makrut (kaffir lime) leaves, torn in half
2^1/$_2$ tablespoons fish sauce
1 tablespoon grated palm sugar (jaggery) or soft brown sugar
1 handful Thai sweet basil, to garnish
1 long red chilli, seeded and thinly sliced, to garnish

SERVES 4–6

Trim the chicken of any fat, then cut each thigh into 5 cm (2 inch) pieces. Put the chicken, curry paste, coconut milk, eggplant and four of the lime leaves in the slow cooker. Cook on high for 2 hours, or until the chicken is tender and cooked through.

Stir through the fish sauce, sugar and remaining lime leaves. Garnish with basil and chilli and serve with steamed rice.

PREPARATION TIME: 20 MINUTES   COOKING TIME: 2 HOURS

Chicken braised with ginger and star anise

PENANG CHICKEN CURRY

RED CURRY PASTE
1 red onion, thickly sliced
10 g (¼ oz) galangal, sliced
2 garlic cloves, chopped
1 teaspoon chilli powder
2 coriander (cilantro) roots, washed well
1 teaspoon shrimp paste
3 tablespoons peanuts, toasted

800 g (1 lb 12 oz) boneless, skinless
chicken breasts
400 ml (14 fl oz) tinned coconut cream
coriander (cilantro) leaves, to garnish
sliced red chilli, to garnish

SERVES 4

To make the red curry paste, place all the paste ingredients in a food processor and blend until smooth. Alternatively, pound the ingredients using a mortar and pestle to form a smooth paste.

Trim the chicken of any fat, then chop into 2 cm (3/4 inch) pieces and put in a large bowl. Add the red curry paste and mix well to coat the chicken in the paste.

Put the chicken in the slow cooker. Cook on high for 2 hours, then add the coconut cream and cook for a further 1 hour. Ladle the curry into large serving bowls and garnish with the coriander leaves and chilli. Serve with jasmine rice.

PREPARATION TIME: 10 MINUTES   COOKING TIME: 3 HOURS

CHICKEN AND PRUNE TAGINE

800 g (1 lb 12 oz) boneless, skinless chicken thighs

1 onion, chopped

1/4 teaspoon ground saffron threads

1/2 teaspoon ground ginger

2 cinnamon sticks

4 coriander (cilantro) sprigs, tied in a bunch

zest of 1/2 lemon, removed in wide strips

300 g (10 1/2 oz/1 1/3 cups) pitted prunes

2 tablespoons honey

1 tablespoon sesame seeds, toasted

SERVES 4

Trim the chicken of any fat, then cut each thigh into quarters. Put the chicken pieces, onion, saffron, ginger, cinnamon sticks, bunch of coriander sprigs and 250 ml (9 fl oz/1 cup) water in the slow cooker. Cook on high for 2 1/2 hours, or until the chicken is tender.

Add the strips of lemon zest, prunes and honey, cover and cook for a further 30 minutes, or until the chicken is very tender and cooked through. Remove and discard the coriander sprigs. Serve hot, sprinkled with sesame seeds.

PREPARATION TIME: 15 MINUTES   COOKING TIME: 3 HOURS

BUTTER CHICKEN

1 kg (2 lb 4 oz) boneless, skinless chicken thighs

2 teaspoons garam masala

2 teaspoons sweet paprika

2 teaspoons ground coriander

1 tablespoon grated fresh ginger

1/4 teaspoon chilli powder

1 cinnamon stick

6 cardamom pods, bruised

375 g (13 oz/1 1/2 cups) tomato passata (puréed tomatoes)

60 g (2 1/4 oz/1/4 cup) plain yoghurt

2 tablespoons cornflour (cornstarch)

1 tablespoon sugar

125 ml (4 fl oz/1/2 cup) pouring cream

1 tablespoon lemon juice

SERVES 6

Trim the chicken of any fat, then cut each thigh into quarters. Put the chicken pieces, garam masala, paprika, coriander, ginger, chilli, cinnamon stick, cardamom and tomato passata in the slow cooker. Cook on low for 4 hours, or until the chicken is tender and cooked through.

Combine the yoghurt with the cornflour. Turn the slow cooker heat to high. Add the yoghurt mixture to the slow cooker along with the sugar, cream and lemon juice. Cook for a further 10 minutes, or until the sauce has thickened slightly. Serve with steamed rice.

PREPARATION TIME: 20 MINUTES   COOKING TIME: 4 1/4 HOURS

Chicken and prune tagine

Nov 30/09   4/5 stars says Joe
Next time add more liquid → should be more saucy (ie orange
could ↓ sugar (esp. if BBque sauce is sweet)   apple juice
3/4 c)

PORK WITH ONION AND
BARBECUE SAUCE

250 g (9 oz/1 cup) barbecue sauce
1 1/2 tablespoons roughly chopped
jalapeño chilli
1/2 teaspoon ground cumin
1/4 teaspoon ground cinnamon
1 teaspoon paprika
45 g (1 1/2 oz/1/4 cup) soft brown sugar
2 garlic cloves, chopped
1 teaspoon dijon mustard
2 tablepoons red wine vinegar
2 teaspoons worcestershire sauce
1 onion, thinly sliced
1.6 kg (3 lb 8 oz) boned, rolled pork loin
1 tablespoon coriander (cilantro)
leaves, chopped
bread rolls, to serve

SERVES 4–6

Put the barbecue sauce, jalapeño, cumin, cinnamon, paprika, brown
sugar, garlic, mustard, vinegar and worcestershire sauce in a bowl. Add
250 ml (9 fl oz/1 cup) water and stir to combine.

Put the onion in the base of the slow cooker. Add the pork and pour the
sauce over the top. Cook on high for 7 hours, or until the pork is tender.
When the pork is cool enough to handle, shred the meat apart using two
forks or your fingers. Stir in the chopped coriander.

Serve the pork topped with the onion and barbecue sauce on fresh
bread rolls. Serve with a side salad if desired.
↑ to 2 onions next time.

PREPARATION TIME: 20 MINUTES   COOKING TIME: 7 HOURS
used Thai basil & parsley

JAPANESE SLOW-COOKED PORK BELLY

1 kg (2 lb 4 oz) boneless pork belly
100 g (3^1/$_2$ oz) fresh ginger, cut into thick slices
500 ml (17 fl oz/2 cups) dashi (made up according to packet instructions)
170 ml (5^1/$_2$ fl oz/^{2}/$_3$ cup) sake
60 ml (2 fl oz/^{1}/$_4$ cup) mirin
80 g (2^3/$_4$ oz/^{1}/$_3$ cup firmly packed) dark brown sugar
125 ml (4 fl oz/^{1}/$_2$ cup) Japanese soy sauce
Japanese mustard, to serve (optional)

SERVES 4–6

Cut the pork into 5 cm (2 inch) cubes. Put the pork, ginger, dashi, sake, mirin, brown sugar and soy sauce in the slow cooker. Pour in 375 ml (13 fl oz/1^1/$_2$ cups) water. Cook on low for 4^1/$_2$ hours, or until the pork is tender.

Remove the lid and increase the slow cooker heat to high. Cook for a further 30 minutes, or until the sauce is slightly reduced. Serve with Japanese mustard on the side if desired and steamed rice.

PREPARATION TIME: 20 MINUTES   COOKING TIME: 5 HOURS

ADOBE PORK

1 kg (2 lb 4 oz) pork neck
1 red onion, sliced
2 garlic cloves, chopped
125 ml (4 fl oz/^{1}/$_2$ cup) light soy sauce
1^1/$_2$ tablespoons apple cider vinegar
250 ml (9 fl oz/1 cup) beef stock
2 tablespoons soft brown sugar
1 tablespoon shredded fresh ginger
2 bay leaves
2 tablespoons plain (all-purpose) flour
1^1/$_2$ tablespoons lime juice

SERVES 6

Cut the pork into 4 cm (1^1/$_2$ inch) pieces. Combine the pork, onion, garlic, soy sauce, vinegar, stock, brown sugar, ginger, bay leaves and flour in the slow cooker. Cook on high for 4 hours, or until the pork is tender.

Remove the lid and cook for a further 30 minutes, or until the sauce has thickened slightly.

Stir through the lime juice and season to taste with salt and freshly ground black pepper. Serve with steamed rice.

PREPARATION TIME: 20 MINUTES   COOKING TIME: 4^1/$_2$ HOURS

Japanese slow-cooked pork belly

PORK VINDALOO

Used pork tenderloin

800 g (1 lb 12 oz) boneless pork leg
6 cardamom pods
1 teaspoon black peppercorns
4 dried chillies
1 teaspoon cloves
10 cm (4 inch) piece cinnamon stick, roughly broken
1 teaspoon cumin seeds
1/2 teaspoon coriander seeds
1/4 teaspoon fenugreek seeds
1/2 teaspoon ground turmeric
80 ml (2 1/2 fl oz/1/3 cup) white wine vinegar
1 tablespoon balsamic vinegar
2 onions, thinly sliced
10 garlic cloves, thinly sliced
5 cm (2 inch) piece fresh ginger, cut into matchsticks
250 g (9 oz/1 cup) tomato passata (puréed tomatoes)
4 green chillies, seeded and chopped
1 teaspoon grated palm sugar (jaggery) or soft brown sugar

SERVES 4

Trim the pork leg of any excess fat and cut the meat into 2.5 cm (1 inch) cubes. Set aside while you make the marinade.

Split open the cardamom pods and remove the seeds. Using a mortar and pestle or a spice grinder, finely pound or grind the cardamom seeds, peppercorns, dried chillies, cloves, cinnamon stick, cumin seeds, coriander seeds, fenugreek seeds and turmeric.

In a large bowl, mix the ground spices together with the vinegars. Add the pork and mix thoroughly to coat well. Cover and marinate in the refrigerator for 3 hours.

Combine the pork, onion, garlic, ginger, tomato passata, chilli and sugar in the slow cooker. Cook on high for 3 1/2 hours, or until the pork is very tender. Serve with steamed rice.

PREPARATION TIME: 25 MINUTES +   COOKING TIME: 3 1/2 HOURS

RED-COOKED PORK BELLY

1 kg (2 lb 4 oz) pork belly
500 ml (17 fl oz/2 cups) chicken stock
60 ml (2 fl oz/1/4 cup) dark soy sauce
60 ml (2 fl oz/1/4 cup) Chinese rice wine
6 dried shiitake mushrooms
4 garlic cloves, bruised
5 x 5 cm (2 x 2 inch) piece fresh ginger, sliced
1 piece dried mandarin or tangerine peel
2 teaspoons sichuan peppercorns
2 star anise
1 cinnamon stick
2 tablespoons Chinese rock sugar (see Note)
1 teaspoon sesame oil
3 spring onions (scallions), thinly sliced diagonally

SERVES 6

Put the pork belly, stock, soy sauce, rice wine, mushrooms, garlic, ginger, mandarin peel, peppercorns, star anise, cinnamon stick, rock sugar and sesame oil in the slow cooker. Cook on low for 6 hours, or until the pork is very tender. Remove the pork from the stock and set aside.

Strain the liquid into a bowl, set the mushrooms aside, then return the strained liquid to the slow cooker. Increase the heat to high and cook, uncovered, for a further 1 hour, or until the liquid has reduced and thickened. About 15 minutes before the end of cooking time, return the pork and mushrooms to the slow cooker to heat through.

Remove the pork from the stock and cut into 1 cm (1/2 inch) thick slices. Transfer to a platter with the mushrooms and spoon over some of the cooking liquid. Sprinkle over the spring onions and serve with rice.

PREPARATION TIME: 15 MINUTES   COOKING TIME: 7 HOURS

NOTE: Chinese rock sugar is a crystallised form of pure sugar and is named for its irregular rock-shaped pieces. It imparts a rich flavour, especially to braised or 'red-cooked' foods, and gives them a translucent glaze. Rock sugar is sold in Asian grocery stores.

MA PO TOFU WITH PORK

2 tablespoons fermented black beans
400 g (14 oz) minced (ground) pork
1 tablespoon finely chopped fresh ginger
3 spring onions (scallions), finely chopped
125 ml (4 fl oz/$^1/_2$ cup) chicken stock
2 tablespoons soy sauce
1 tablespoon chilli bean paste
2 tablespoons Chinese rice wine
450 g (1 lb) firm tofu, cut into
1.5 cm ($^5/_8$ inch) cubes
2 garlic cloves, chopped
1 tablespoon cornflour (cornstarch)
2 teaspoons sesame oil
spring onions (scallions), extra, sliced
diagonally, to serve

SERVES 4–6

Put the black beans in a bowl of cold water and soak for 5 minutes. Drain and finely chop.

Put the beans, pork, ginger, spring onion, stock, soy sauce, chilli bean paste and rice wine in the slow cooker. Cook on low for 2 hours.

Add the tofu and garlic and stir gently until the tofu is well coated with the sauce. Cook for a further 20–30 minutes, or until the mixture has thickened. Garnish with the extra spring onions and serve with rice.

PREPARATION TIME: 20 MINUTES   COOKING TIME: 2$^1/_2$ HOURS

MUSSAMAN CURRY

800 g (1 lb 12 oz) chuck steak
2 cinnamon sticks
10 cardamom seeds
5 cloves
2 tablespoons mussaman curry paste
250 ml (9 fl oz/1 cup) coconut milk
2–3 all-purpose potatoes, cut into
2.5 cm (1 inch) pieces
2 cm ($^3/_4$ inch) piece fresh ginger,
shredded
60 ml (2 fl oz/$^1/_4$ cup) fish sauce
60 ml (2 fl oz/$^1/_4$ cup) grated palm sugar
(jaggery) or soft brown sugar
110 g (3$^3/_4$ oz/$^2/_3$ cup) roasted
salted peanuts
3 tablespoons tamarind purée

SERVES 4

Trim the beef and cut into 5 cm (2 inch) cubes. Put the beef, cinnamon sticks, cardamom, cloves, curry paste, coconut milk, potato, ginger, fish sauce, sugar, three-quarters of the roasted peanuts and the tamarind purée in the slow cooker. Cook on high for 4 hours, or until the beef is tender and the potato is just cooked.

Taste, then adjust the seasoning with salt and freshly ground black pepper if necessary. Spoon into serving bowls and garnish with the remaining roasted peanuts. Serve with steamed rice.

PREPARATION TIME: 20 MINUTES   COOKING TIME: 4 HOURS

SICHUAN AND ANISE BEEF STEW

1 kg (2 lb 4 oz) chuck steak
1¹/₂ tablespoons plain (all-purpose) flour
1 large red onion, thickly sliced
2 garlic cloves, crushed
3 tablespoons tomato paste
(concentrated purée)
250 ml (9 fl oz/1 cup) red wine
250 ml (9 fl oz/1 cup) beef stock
2 bay leaves, crushed
3 long strips orange zest, about
1.5 cm (⁵/₈ inch) wide
2 star anise
1 teaspoon sichuan peppercorns
1 teaspoon chopped thyme
1 tablespoon chopped rosemary
3 tablespoons chopped coriander
(cilantro) leaves

SERVES 4

Trim the beef and cut into 3 cm (1¹/₄ inch) cubes. Put the beef, flour, onion, garlic, tomato paste, wine, stock, bay leaves, strips of orange zest, star anise, peppercorns, thyme and rosemary in the slow cooker. Cook on high for 3 hours, or until the beef is tender.

Season to taste with salt and freshly ground black pepper. Stir in most of the coriander leaves and garnish with the remainder. Serve the stew with steamed rice.

PREPARATION TIME: 20 MINUTES   COOKING TIME: 3 HOURS

SAAG LAMB

1 kg (2 lb 4 oz) boneless lamb leg
or shoulder
1 teaspoon fenugreek seeds
1 teaspoon cumin seeds
1 teaspoon mustard seeds
2 onions, diced
2 garlic cloves, finely chopped
2 teaspoons grated fresh ginger
2 small red chillies, seeded and
finely diced
2 cinnamon sticks
4 fresh curry leaves
250 ml (9 fl oz/1 cup) beef stock
400 g (14 oz) baby English spinach

CORIANDER YOGHURT
125 g (4^{1}/$_2$ oz/^{1}/$_2$ cup) Greek-style yoghurt
1 tablespoon lemon juice
1 small handful coriander (cilantro)
leaves, chopped

SERVES 4

Trim the lamb of excess fat, then cut into 3 cm (1^{1}/$_4$ inch) cubes. Put the lamb in a large bowl.

Using a mortar and pestle or spice grinder, pound or grind the fenugreek, cumin and mustard seeds. Combine the ground spices with the onion, garlic, ginger and chilli. Stir the spice mixture into the lamb, stirring well to coat the lamb with the spices. Cover and leave to marinate in the refrigerator overnight.

Put the lamb, cinnamon sticks, curry leaves and stock in the slow cooker. Cook on high for 4 hours, then add the spinach and cook for a further 1 hour, or until the lamb is tender.

Meanwhile, to make the coriander yoghurt, combine the yoghurt, lemon juice and coriander. Serve the lamb with the coriander yoghurt and steamed basmati rice.

PREPARATION TIME: 30 MINUTES +   COOKING TIME: 5 HOURS

LAMB MADRAS

1 kg (2 lb 4 oz) boneless lamb leg
or shoulder
60 g (2^1/$_4$ oz/^{1}/$_4$ cup) madras curry paste
1 onion, finely chopped
6 cardamom pods
4 cloves
2 bay leaves
1 cinnamon stick
185 g (6^1/$_2$ oz/^{3}/$_4$ cup) Greek-style
yoghurt
^{1}/$_4$ teaspoon garam masala
2 long red chillies, chopped (optional)

SERVES 4

Trim the lamb of excess fat and cut into 3 cm (1^1/$_4$ inch) cubes. Combine the curry paste and lamb in a large bowl and stir thoroughly to coat. Cover and marinate for at least 2 hours, or overnight, in the refrigerator.

Put the marinated lamb, onion, cardamom pods, cloves, bay leaves, cinnamon stick and yoghurt in the slow cooker. Cook on high for 4 hours, or until the lamb is tender and cooked through. Season with salt and sprinkle with the garam masala. Garnish with chilli if desired and serve with rice.

PREPARATION TIME: 25 MINUTES +   COOKING TIME: 4 HOURS

LAMB WITH GREEN OLIVES AND PRESERVED LEMON

1/2 preserved lemon
1 kg (2 lb 4 oz) lamb forequarter chops
1 onion, sliced
2 garlic cloves, crushed
2 cm (3/4 inch) piece fresh ginger,
finely diced
1 teaspoon ground cumin
1/2 teaspoon ground turmeric
130 g (4 1/2 oz/3/4 cup) green olives
625 ml (21 fl oz/2 1/2 cups) chicken stock
400 g (14 oz) all-purpose potatoes,
cut into 2 cm (3/4 inch) dice
2 tablespoons chopped flat-leaf
(Italian) parsley
2 tablespoons chopped coriander
(cilantro) leaves

SERVES 4

Rinse the preserved lemon well, remove and discard the pulp and membrane and finely dice the rind.

Trim the lamb of any excess fat and cut each chop in half.

Put the lemon, lamb chops, onion, garlic, ginger, cumin, turmeric, olives and stock in the slow cooker. Cook on high for 2 hours. Add the potato and half the combined parsley and coriander leaves and cook for a further 1 hour, or until the lamb is tender and the potato is cooked.

Stir through the remaining parsley and coriander and season to taste with salt and freshly ground black pepper. Serve with rice.

PREPARATION TIME: 30 MINUTES   COOKING TIME: 3 HOURS

LAMB KORMA

1 kg (2 lb 4 oz) boneless lamb leg or shoulder
2 tablespoons Greek-style yoghurt
60 g (2¼ oz/¼ cup) korma paste
2 onions
2 tablespoons desiccated coconut
3 green chillies, roughly chopped
4 garlic cloves, crushed
5 cm (2 inch) piece fresh ginger, grated
50 g (1¾ oz/⅓ cup) cashew nuts
6 cloves
¼ teaspoon ground cinnamon
125 ml (4 fl oz/½ cup) chicken stock
6 cardamom pods, crushed
2 tablespoons pouring cream
1 handful coriander (cilantro) leaves, to garnish

Trim the lamb of excess fat and cut into 2.5 cm (1 inch) cubes. Put the lamb in a bowl, add the yoghurt and korma paste and mix to coat the lamb thoroughly.

Roughly chop one onion and thinly slice the other. Put the roughly chopped onion, coconut, chilli, garlic, ginger, cashew nuts, cloves and cinnamon in the bowl of a food processor. Add the stock and process to form a smooth paste. Alternatively, finely chop the ingredients with a knife before adding the stock.

Put the lamb, spice mixture, sliced onion, cardamom and a pinch of salt in the slow cooker. Cook on high for 3 hours, or until the lamb is tender. Stir through the cream and cook for a further 10 minutes. Season to taste with salt and freshly ground black pepper.

Ladle the curry into serving bowls over steamed rice and sprinkle with the coriander leaves.

SERVES 4–6   PREPARATION TIME: 20 MINUTES   COOKING TIME: 3¼ HOURS

AFRICAN STYLE LAMB AND PEANUT STEW

1 kg (2 lb 4 oz) lamb (such as boneless lamb leg steaks)

3 teaspoons curry powder

1 teaspoon dried oregano

pinch cayenne pepper

1 large onion, chopped

1 large carrot, chopped

1 red capsicum (pepper), seeded and chopped

500 g (1 lb 2 oz) orange sweet potato, cut into 2 cm (^{3}/$_4$ inch) cubes

4 garlic cloves, chopped

1 red or green chilli, seeded and finely chopped

400 g (14 oz) tinned chopped tomatoes

125 ml (4 fl oz/^{1}/$_2$ cup) tomato sauce (ketchup)

2 bay leaves

90 g (3^1/$_4$ oz/^{1}/$_3$ cup) crunchy or smooth peanut butter

1 tablespoon lemon juice

165 ml (5^1/$_2$ fl oz) tinned coconut milk

155 g (5^1/$_2$ oz/1 cup) fresh or frozen peas

SERVES 4–6

Trim the lamb of any fat and cut into 2 cm (^{3}/$_4$ inch) cubes. Put the lamb in a large bowl and sprinkle over the curry powder, oregano and cayenne pepper. Season with salt and freshly ground black pepper. Toss well to coat the lamb.

Add the onion, carrot, capsicum, sweet potato, garlic, chilli, tomatoes, tomato sauce and bay leaves to the lamb. Toss to thoroughly combine all the ingredients. Transfer the lamb and vegetables to the slow cooker. Cook on high for 4–6 hours, or until the lamb and vegetables are tender and cooked through.

Meanwhile, combine the peanut butter, lemon juice and coconut milk in a small bowl. During the last 30 minutes of cooking, add the peanut butter mixture to the slow cooker and stir to combine the ingredients. Add the peas and cook for 5 minutes, or until tender.

Remove the bay leaves. Divide the stew among bowls and serve with steamed rice or couscous.

PREPARATION TIME: 30 MINUTES   COOKING TIME: 4–6 HOURS

INDIAN SPICED LEG OF LAMB

1 onion, roughly chopped

4 garlic cloves

4 cm (1¹/₂ inch) piece fresh ginger, diced

2 tablespoons chopped coriander (cilantro) leaves

¹/₂ teaspoon ground cinnamon

¹/₂ teaspoon cardamom seeds

2 teaspoons ground cumin

¹/₂ teaspoon ground dried chillies

1 teaspoon ground turmeric

¹/₂ teaspoon garam masala

2 teaspoons curry powder

300 g (10¹/₂ oz) plain yoghurt

juice of ¹/₂ lemon

1.2 kg (2 lb 10 oz) lamb leg

2 egg yolks

SERVES 4–6

Put the onion, garlic, ginger and coriander in the bowl of a food processor and process until smooth. Add the cinnamon, cardamom seeds, cumin, chilli, turmeric, garam masala, curry powder and a pinch of salt. Process until combined. Stir in 200 g (7 oz) of the yoghurt and the lemon juice.

Wash and dry the lamb. Cut slits in the side of the lamb, then coat the lamb in the yoghurt mixture, filling the slits. Cover with plastic wrap and place in the refrigerator to marinate for 24 hours.

Put the lamb and the marinade in the slow cooker. Cook on low for 7 hours, or until the lamb is tender and cooked. Remove the lamb, cover and set aside.

Combine the remaining yoghurt and the egg yolks. Stir into the liquid in the slow cooker and cook for 20–30 minutes, stirring occasionally, until the sauce has thickened slightly. Return the lamb to the slow cooker and cook for a further 10 minutes. Carve the lamb and serve with the sauce and steamed rice.

PREPARATION TIME: 30 MINUTES +   COOKING TIME: 7³/4 HOURS

MOROCCAN SPICED LAMB WITH PUMPKIN

1.5 kg (3 lb 5 oz) boneless lamb shoulder
1 large onion, diced
1 teaspoon ground coriander
$^1/_2$ teaspoon ground ginger
$^1/_2$ teaspoon cayenne pepper
$^1/_4$ teaspoon ground saffron threads
1 cinnamon stick
500 ml (17 fl oz/2 cups) chicken stock
500 g (1 lb 2 oz) pumpkin (winter squash),
cut into 2 cm ($^3/_4$ inch) dice
100 g (3$^1/_2$ oz) dried apricots
coriander (cilantro) sprigs, to garnish

SERVES 6

Trim the lamb of excess fat and cut into 3 cm (1$^1/_4$ inch) cubes. Put the lamb, onion, ground coriander, ginger, cayenne pepper, saffron, cinnamon stick, stock and pumpkin in the slow cooker. Cook on low for 4 hours. Add the apricots and cook for a further 1 hour.

Taste the sauce and adjust the seasoning with salt and freshly ground black pepper if necessary. Transfer to a warm serving dish and garnish with the coriander sprigs. Serve with couscous or rice.

PREPARATION TIME: 20 MINUTES   COOKING TIME: 5 HOURS

LAMB SHANKS WITH TOMATO, CHILLI AND HONEY

8 lamb shanks, French trimmed
2 garlic cloves, thinly sliced
1 large onion, sliced
250 ml (9 fl oz/1 cup) red wine
2 teaspoons dried oregano
$^1/_2$ teaspoon chilli flakes
500 g (1 lb 2 oz/2 cups) tomato passata
(puréed tomatoes)
250 ml (9 fl oz/1 cup) chicken stock
90 g (3$^1/_4$ oz/$^1/_4$ cup) honey
1 tablespoon chopped flat-leaf
(Italian) parsley

SERVES 4

Put the lamb shanks, garlic, onion, wine, oregano, chilli flakes, tomato passata, stock and honey in the slow cooker. Cook on low for 8 hours, or until the shanks are tender.

Stir through the parsley and season with salt and freshly ground black pepper. Serve with steamed rice.

PREPARATION TIME: 15 MINUTES   COOKING TIME: 8 HOURS

Moroccan spiced lamb with pumpkin

ROGAN JOSH

1 kg (2 lb 4 oz) boneless lamb leg
or shoulder
3 garlic cloves, crushed
6 cm (2¹/₂ inch) piece fresh ginger, grated
2 teaspoons ground cumin
1 teaspoon chilli powder
2 teaspoons paprika
2 teaspoons ground coriander
1 onion, finely chopped
6 cardamom pods, crushed
4 cloves
2 bay leaves
1 cinnamon stick
200 g (7 oz) plain yoghurt
4 saffron threads
2 tablespoons milk
¹/₂ teaspoon garam masala
coriander (cilantro) sprigs, to garnish

SERVES 6

Trim the lamb of excess fat and cut into 4 cm (1¹/₂ inch) cubes.

Mix together the garlic, ginger, cumin, chilli powder, paprika and ground coriander in a large bowl. Add the lamb and stir thoroughly to coat the lamb in the spices. Cover and marinate in the refrigerator for at least 2 hours, or overnight.

Put the lamb mixture in the slow cooker. Stir in the onion, cardamom, cloves, bay leaves, cinnamon stick, yoghurt and 60 ml (2 fl oz/¹/₄ cup) water. Cook on low for 6 hours, or until the lamb is tender.

Meanwhile, combine the saffron with the milk and set aside to soak for 10 minutes. Just before the end of cooking time, stir the saffron and milk mixture, along with the garam masala, into the lamb in the slow cooker. Season to taste with salt. Serve the curry with steamed rice and garnish with coriander sprigs.

PREPARATION TIME: 20 MINUTES +   COOKING TIME: 6 HOURS

PULSES AND GRAINS

POLENTA AND VEGETABLE HOTPOT

2 tablespoons olive oil
300 g (10^1/2 oz/2 cups) polenta
^{1}/4 teaspoon paprika
pinch cayenne pepper
1.5 litres (52 fl oz/6 cups) vegetable stock or water
3 spring onions (scallions), chopped
1 large tomato, chopped
1 zucchini (courgette), chopped
1 red or green capsicum (pepper), seeded and chopped
300 g (10^1/2 oz) pumpkin (winter squash), peeled and cut into 1.5 cm (^{5}/8 inch) dice
100 g (3^1/2 oz) button mushrooms, chopped
300 g (10^1/2 oz) tinned corn kernels, drained
100 g (3^1/2 oz/1 cup) freshly grated parmesan cheese
1 handful flat-leaf (Italian) parsley, chopped
125 ml (4 fl oz/^{1}/2 cup) pouring cream (optional)

SERVES 4–6

Pour 1 tablespoon of the olive oil into the slow cooker bowl and spread it over the base and side. Pour in the polenta, then add the paprika, cayenne pepper, 1 teaspoon salt and some freshly ground black pepper. Stir in the stock and remaining oil. Stir to combine.

Add the spring onion, tomato, zucchini, capsicum, pumpkin, mushrooms and corn and mix well. Cook on high for 2–3 hours, or until the polenta is soft and the vegetables are cooked. Stir several times with a fork to keep the polenta from setting on the base. Start checking after 2 hours to see if the vegetables are tender.

Before serving, stir through the parmesan and parsley. For a richer taste, stir through the cream. Taste and season with extra salt and freshly ground black pepper if necessary. Serve with a green salad.

PREPARATION TIME: 20 MINUTES   COOKING TIME: 2–3 HOURS

NOTE: You can also serve this vegetable hotpot as an accompaniment to barbecued meats.

KEDGEREE

500 g (1 lb 2 oz/2¹/₂ cups) par-cooked long-grain rice
1 onion, finely chopped
2 tablespoons mild Indian curry paste
1 teaspoon ground cumin
2 bay leaves
500 ml (17 fl oz/2 cups) chicken or fish stock
500 g (1 lb 2 oz) boneless, skinless salmon fillets
125 ml (4 fl oz/¹/₂ cup) pouring cream
50 g (1³/₄ oz) butter
155 g (5¹/₂ oz/1 cup) fresh or frozen peas
2 tablespoons chopped flat-leaf (Italian) parsley
2 tablespoons lemon juice

SERVES 4

Put the rice, onion, curry paste, cumin and bay leaves in the slow cooker. Pour over the stock and 250 ml (9 fl oz/1 cup) water. Cook on low for 2¹/₂ hours, or until the rice is almost tender.

Meanwhile, prepare the salmon. Check for any bones and remove with your fingers or tweezers. Cut the salmon into 3 cm (1¹/₄ inch) cubes.

Put the salmon on top of the rice, add the cream, butter and peas and cook for a further 30 minutes, or until the rice is tender and the fish is cooked. Stir through the parsley and lemon juice and season with salt and freshly ground black pepper.

PREPARATION TIME: 15 MINUTES   COOKING TIME: 3 HOURS

ARMENIAN CHICKEN WITH RICE PILAFF

cooking oil spray

1.2 kg (2 lb 10 oz) chicken

1 lemon

2 garlic cloves, lightly crushed

3 thyme sprigs

2 teaspoons olive oil

1/4 teaspoon paprika

RICE PILAFF

200 g (7 oz/1 cup) par-cooked long-grain rice

50 g (1³/4 oz) vermicelli, broken into small pieces

40 g (1¹/2 oz/¹/4 cup) pine nuts

30 g (1 oz) butter, melted

500 ml (17 fl oz/2 cups) chicken stock

SERVES 4

Spray the slow cooker bowl with cooking oil spray or grease well with butter or oil.

Wash the chicken and pat dry with paper towel. Finely grate the zest from half of the lemon and set the zest aside. Cut the lemon into quarters. Stuff the chicken with the lemon quarters, garlic and thyme. Skewer or tie the legs and wings together with kitchen string, then place the chicken, breast side up, in the slow cooker.

Brush the chicken breast and legs with the olive oil and sprinkle over the paprika, some salt and freshly ground black pepper. Cook on high for 1 hour.

Meanwhile, to make the rice pilaff, put the rice, vermicelli and pine nuts in a large bowl and stir through the butter and reserved lemon zest, then add the chicken stock. Carefully pour this around the chicken in the slow cooker, distributing it evenly around and mixing the rice and vermicelli into the liquid.

Cook on high for a further 3-4 hours, or until the rice is cooked and the chicken is tender and the juices run clear when the thigh is pierced with a skewer. Stir the rice with a fork once or twice during cooking.

Lift the chicken carefully from the slow cooker and remove the skewers or string. Cut or pull the chicken apart into large pieces. Serve with the rice pilaff and a salad or steamed vegetables.

PREPARATION TIME: 25 MINUTES   COOKING TIME: 4–5 HOURS

MILD CURRY OF CHICKEN, SWEET POTATOES AND SPLIT PEAS

220 g (7³/4 oz/1 cup) dried yellow split peas
2 boneless, skinless chicken breasts
1 tablespoon vegetable oil
1 red onion, chopped
2 garlic cloves, crushed
1 tablespoon grated fresh ginger
3 teaspoons curry powder
500 g (1 lb 2 oz) orange sweet potato, cut into 2 cm (³/4 inch) cubes
100 g (3¹/2 oz) green beans, trimmed and cut into 4 cm (1¹/2 inch) lengths
400 g (14 oz) tinned chopped tomatoes
250 ml (9 fl oz/1 cup) chicken stock
125 ml (4 fl oz/¹/2 cup) pouring cream
1 small handful coriander (cilantro) leaves, chopped

SERVES 4–6

Put the split peas in a bowl, cover with plenty of water and soak for several hours or overnight. Drain.

Trim the chicken of any fat and cut into 2 cm (³/4 inch) cubes.

Pour the oil into the slow cooker bowl and spread over the base and side. Add the onion, garlic and ginger and stir in the curry powder. Add the split peas, chicken, sweet potato and beans. Pour over the tomatoes and stock and season well with salt and freshly ground black pepper.

Cook on high for 3–4 hours, or until the split peas and sweet potato are cooked. Stir occasionally during the cooking time. Just before serving, stir in the cream and chopped coriander and heat through for a few minutes. Serve with basmati rice.

PREPARATION TIME: 20 MINUTES + COOKING TIME: 3–4 HOURS

DRUNKEN CHICKEN WITH RICE

1.6 kg (3 lb 8 oz) chicken
2 slices fresh ginger
2 garlic cloves, squashed
2 spring onions (scallions), trimmed
1 star anise
250 g (9 oz/1¼ cups) par-cooked long-grain rice
250 ml (9 fl oz/1 cup) Chinese rice wine
250 ml (9 fl oz/1 cup) chicken stock
light soy sauce, to serve

SERVES 4

Trim the excess fat from the cavity of the chicken. Put the ginger, garlic, spring onions and star anise in the cavity.

Put the rice in the base of the slow cooker. Pour over the rice wine and stock and place the chicken on the top. Cook on high for 3 hours, or until the rice is cooked and the chicken juices run clear when the thigh is pierced with a skewer. Serve drizzled with light soy sauce.

PREPARATION TIME: 15 MINUTES   COOKING TIME: 3 HOURS

MEXICAN CHICKEN

cooking oil spray
600 g (1 lb 5 oz) boneless, skinless chicken thighs
330 g (11½ oz/1½ cups) par-cooked short-grain rice
400 g (14 oz) tinned red kidney beans, drained and rinsed
400 g (14 oz) jar spicy taco sauce
250 ml (9 fl oz/1 cup) chicken stock
250 g (9 oz/2 cups) grated cheddar cheese
125 g (4½ oz/½ cup) sour cream
1 handful coriander (cilantro) leaves, chopped

SERVES 4

Spray the slow cooker bowl with cooking oil spray or grease well with butter or oil.

Trim the chicken of excess fat and cut each thigh in half. Put the rice in the base of the slow cooker and top with the chicken pieces, kidney beans, taco sauce, stock and cheese. Cook on low for 4 hours, or until the chicken and rice are tender.

Serve the chicken topped with a dollop of sour cream and garnish with chopped coriander.

PREPARATION TIME: 10 MINUTES   COOKING TIME: 4 HOURS

ARROZ CON POLLO

4 very ripe tomatoes
2 kg (4 lb 8 oz) chicken pieces, skin removed
100 g (3¹/₂ oz) chorizo sausage, sliced
1 large onion, finely chopped
1 green capsicum (pepper), seeded and diced
1 tablespoon sweet paprika
1 long red chilli, seeded and finely chopped
2 garlic cloves, crushed
pinch saffron threads (optional)
250 ml (9 fl oz/1 cup) chicken stock
2¹/₂ tablespoons tomato paste (concentrated purée)
80 ml (2¹/₂ fl oz/¹/₃ cup) sherry
400 g (14 oz/2 cups) par-cooked rice
100 g (3¹/₂ oz/²/₃ cup) frozen peas
3 tablespoons finely chopped flat-leaf (Italian) parsley
55 g (2 oz/¹/₃ cup) stuffed green olives (optional)

SERVES 6

Score a cross in the base of each tomato. Put the tomatoes in a heatproof bowl and cover with boiling water. Leave for 30 seconds, then transfer to cold water, drain and peel the skin away from the cross. Cut the tomatoes in half, scoop out the seeds with a teaspoon and roughly chop the flesh.

Put the tomato, chicken pieces, chorizo, onion, capsicum, paprika, chilli, garlic, saffron (if using), stock, tomato paste and sherry in the slow cooker. Cook on low for 8 hours.

Add the rice to the slow cooker and stir to coat well. Cook for a further 1 hour, or until the liquid has absorbed, then stir in the peas, cover and cook for a further 5 minutes, or until the rice, peas and chicken are tender and cooked through.

Stir in the parsley and olives, if using, and season to taste with salt and freshly ground black pepper. Serve immediately.

PREPARATION TIME: 20 MINUTES   COOKING TIME: 9 HOURS

BROWN RICE AND BARLEY RISOTTO WITH PUMPKIN AND CHICKEN

330 g (11^1/2 oz/1^1/2 cups) short-grain brown rice

110 g (3^3/4 oz/^{1}/2 cup) pearl barley

1 boneless, skinless chicken breast

1 tablespoon olive oil

1 red onion, finely chopped

350 g (12 oz) pumpkin (winter squash), peeled, seeded and cut into 1 cm (^{1}/2 inch) dice

12 sage leaves

1 teaspoon vegetable or chicken stock powder (optional)

60 ml (2 fl oz/^{1}/4 cup) white wine

155 g (5^1/2 oz/1 cup) fresh or frozen peas

50 g (1^3/4 oz/^{1}/2 cup) freshly grated parmesan cheese, plus extra, to serve

sage leaves, to serve (optional)

SERVES 4

Put the rice and barley in a bowl and cover with 1 litre (35 fl oz/4 cups) water. Leave to soak for 8 hours, or overnight.

Trim the chicken of excess fat and cut into bite-sized cubes. Pour the olive oil into the slow cooker bowl and spread the oil over the base and side. Pour the rice and barley, along with the soaking water, into the slow cooker. Add the chicken, onion, pumpkin and sage. Mix the stock powder, if using, with the wine, then stir it into the grains. Season well with salt and freshly ground black pepper.

Cook on high for 3 hours, or until all the liquid has been absorbed and the rice and barley are tender. Stir occasionally during the cooking time. If the grains are not quite cooked after 3 hours, cook for a further 20–30 minutes, or until tender.

Before serving, beat the grains with a fork to thoroughly mix in the cooked pumpkin until it looks 'creamy'. Stir in the peas and the parmesan and cook for a further 5 minutes, or until the peas are cooked through.

Season to taste with salt and freshly ground black pepper. Spoon into serving bowls and top with extra grated parmesan cheese and sage leaves if desired.

PREPARATION TIME: 20 MINUTES +   COOKING TIME: 3–3^1/2 HOURS

NOTE: Leave out the chicken and chicken stock for a vegetarian version.

BOSTON-STYLE BAKED BEANS WITH HAM

400 g (14 oz/2 cups) dried cannellini beans
1 large onion, finely chopped
1.5 kg (3 lb 5 oz) ham hock
1 bay leaf
60 ml (2 fl oz/¼ cup) molasses
80 g (2¾ oz/⅓ cup firmly packed) soft brown sugar
160 g (5½ oz/⅔ cup) tomato paste (concentrated purée)
2 tablespoons worcestershire sauce
1 teaspoon mustard powder
1 garlic clove

SERVES 6

Soak the beans in a large saucepan of water overnight. Drain, discarding the water, then put the beans in a saucepan with fresh water, bring to the boil and boil rapidly for 10 minutes. Rinse and drain again.

Put the beans, onion, ham hock, bay leaf, molasses, brown sugar, tomato paste, worcestershire sauce, mustard, garlic and 750 ml (26 fl oz/3 cups) water in the slow cooker. Cook on low for 8–10 hours, or until the beans are soft.

Carefully remove the hock. When cool enough to handle, cut the meat from the bone. Pull the meat apart or cut it into smallish chunks, then return to the slow cooker and stir to combine well. Cook, uncovered, for a further 30 minutes, or until the sauce is thick and syrupy.

Serve the baked beans with thick buttered toast or cornbread to mop up the juices.

PREPARATION TIME: 20 MINUTES +   COOKING TIME: 8–10 HOURS

SPICY SAUSAGE AND BEAN CASSEROLE

300 g (10^1/$_2$ oz/1^1/$_2$ cups) dried
cannellini beans
300 g (10^1/$_2$ oz/1^1/$_3$ cups) dried
black-eyed beans
6 bacon slices, cut into 6 cm (2^1/$_2$ inch)
lengths
4 small onions, quartered
10 garlic cloves, peeled
3 long thin carrots, cut into
3 cm (1^1/$_4$ inch) pieces
3 bay leaves
7 oregano sprigs, leaves only
1 small red chilli, split and seeded
500 ml (17 fl oz/2 cups) chicken stock
2 tablespoons tomato paste
(concentrated purée)
6 thick pork sausages

SERVES 6

Soak the beans in a large saucepan of water overnight. Drain, discarding the water, then put the beans in a saucepan with fresh water, bring to the boil and boil rapidly for 10 minutes. Rinse and drain again.

Layer the bacon over the base of the slow cooker. Add the onion, garlic cloves, carrot, bay leaves, half the oregano and the chilli and season well with freshly ground black pepper. Pour in the cannellini beans and black-eyed beans.

Combine the stock and tomato paste and pour over the beans. Season with freshly ground black pepper. Cook on high for 6 hours, then add the sausages and cook for a further 1^1/$_2$ hours, or until the beans are tender and the sausages are cooked through.

Stir and taste for seasoning. Sprinkle the remaining oregano into the casserole just before serving.

PREPARATION TIME: 20 MINUTES +   COOKING TIME: 7^1/$_2$ HOURS

PORK BELLY WITH VEGETABLES AND LENTILS

1 kg (2 lb 4 oz) pork belly
1 onion
4 cloves
1 large carrot, cut into chunks
200 g (7 oz) swede (rutabaga) or turnips, cut into chunks
100 g (3½ oz) leek, white part only, thickly sliced
1 parsnip, cut into chunks
1 garlic clove
1 bouquet garni
2 bay leaves
6 juniper berries, slightly crushed
350 g (12 oz/1¾ cups) puy lentils or tiny blue-green lentils
2 tablespoons chopped flat-leaf (Italian) parsley

SERVES 6

Slice the pork belly into thick strips. Stud the onion with the cloves. Put the pork strips in the slow cooker along with the studded onion and all the remaining ingredients except the lentils and parsley. Stir thoroughly, then add just enough water to half cover the ingredients. Cook on high for 4 hours.

Put the lentils in a sieve and rinse under cold running water. Add to the slow cooker and cook for a further 1 hour, or until the pork and lentils are tender and cooked through.

Drain the mixture into a colander, discarding the liquid. Return the contents of the colander to the slow cooker, except for the onion, which can be discarded.

Season the pork and lentils with plenty of freshly ground black pepper and taste to see if you need any salt. Just before serving, stir in the chopped parsley.

PREPARATION TIME: 20 MINUTES   COOKING TIME: 5 HOURS

JAMBALAYA

4 vine-ripened tomatoes
1/2 teaspoon saffron threads
1 red onion, sliced
3 bacon slices, rind and fat removed, chopped
2 chorizo sausages, cut into 1 cm (1/2 inch) slices diagonally
1 small red capsicum (pepper), seeded and sliced
1 small green capsicum (pepper), seeded and sliced
2 garlic cloves, finely chopped
1–2 teaspoons seeded, finely chopped jalapeño chilli
1 teaspoon smoked paprika
3 teaspoons Cajun spice mix
400 g (14 oz/2 cups) par-cooked long-grain rice, rinsed
250 ml (9 fl oz/1 cup) beer
500 ml (17 fl oz/2 cups) chicken stock
2 boneless, skinless chicken breasts
16 raw prawns (shrimp)

SERVES 4

Score a cross in the base of each tomato. Put the tomatoes in a heatproof bowl and cover with boiling water. Leave for 30 seconds, then transfer to cold water, drain and peel the skin away from the cross. Cut the tomatoes into quarters and set aside.

Put the saffron in a small bowl with 1 tablespoon warm water and set aside for 10 minutes to soak.

Put the onion, bacon, chorizo, red and green capsicum, garlic, chilli, paprika, Cajun spice mix, rice, beer and stock in the slow cooker. Add the tomato quarters and the saffron and its soaking liquid. Cook on low for 2 hours, or until the rice is tender and the stock is absorbed.

Meanwhile, prepare the chicken and prawns. Trim the chicken of any fat and cut into 1.5 x 6 cm (5/8 x 2 1/2 inch) strips. Peel the prawns, leaving the tails intact. Gently pull out the dark vein from each prawn back, starting at the head end.

Add the chicken and prawns to the slow cooker, stir to combine the ingredients, and cook for a further 1 hour, or until the chicken and prawns are cooked.

PREPARATION TIME: 30 MINUTES   COOKING TIME: 3 HOURS

CASSOULET

4 pork spare ribs (600 g/1 lb 5 oz)
4 thick beef or lamb sausages
6 French shallots, peeled and chopped
1 carrot, diced
1 celery stalk, diced
3–4 garlic cloves, chopped
1/2 teaspoon paprika
1 large rosemary sprig or 1 teaspoon dried rosemary
2 tablespoons tomato paste (concentrated purée)
400 g (14 oz) tinned chopped tomatoes
60 ml (2 fl oz/1/4 cup) white wine
800 g (1 lb 12 oz) tinned white beans, such as cannellini, haricot or butter beans, drained and rinsed
1 small handful flat-leaf (Italian) parsley, chopped

SERVES 4

Prepare the spare ribs by removing the rind and excess fat. Cut each spare rib into three thick chunks. Cut the sausages in half.

Put the ribs, sausages, shallots, carrot, celery and garlic in the slow cooker. Sprinkle over the paprika and tuck in the rosemary sprig (or sprinkle over the dried rosemary). Season with salt and freshly ground black pepper.

Combine the tomato paste with the tomatoes and wine and pour over the meat and vegetables. Stir in the beans.

Cook on low for 6–8 hours, or until the meat is tender. Remove the rosemary sprig and stir through the parsley. Serve the cassoulet with crusty bread.

PREPARATION TIME: 20 MINUTES   COOKING TIME: 6–8 HOURS

PORK AND RICE HOTPOT

500 g (1 lb) lean pork fillet
15 g (¹/₂ oz) dried Chinese mushrooms, sliced
300 g (10 oz/1¹/₂ cups) long-grain rice
1¹/₂ tablespoons hoisin sauce
2 teaspoons grated fresh ginger
3 garlic cloves, crushed
1 cinnamon stick
2 star anise
2 tablespoons dark soy sauce
1 tablespoon light soy sauce
2 tablespoons Chinese rice wine
500 ml (17 fl oz/2 cups) chicken stock
140 g (5 oz) tinned straw mushrooms, rinsed and drained
125 g (4¹/₂ oz) tinned sliced bamboo shoots, drained
shredded spring onions (scallions), to garnish

SERVES 4

Cut the pork into 2 cm (³/₄ inch) cubes. Put the pork, dried mushrooms, rice, hoisin sauce, ginger, garlic, cinnamon stick, star anise, dark and light soy sauces, rice wine, stock, straw mushrooms and bamboo shoots in the slow cooker.

Cook on low for 3 hours, or until the rice and pork are cooked and the stock is absorbed.

Divide the pork and rice among serving bowls, garnish with spring onions and serve with steamed Asian greens.

PREPARATION TIME: 20 MINUTES   COOKING TIME: 3 HOURS

CHILLI BEEF WITH CAPSICUM, CORIANDER AND AVOCADO

800 g (1 lb 12 oz) chuck steak

800 g (1 lb 12 oz) tinned chopped tomatoes

1 red capsicum (pepper), seeded and diced

110 g (3³/4 oz) dark-gilled field mushrooms, finely chopped

2 onions, chopped

2 garlic cloves, crushed

4 medium-hot green chillies, seeded and finely chopped

2 teaspoons ground cumin

¹/2 teaspoon ground cinnamon

1 teaspoon caster (superfine) sugar

2 bay leaves

200 ml (7 fl oz) beef stock

1 large handful coriander (cilantro) leaves

400 g (14 oz) tinned red kidney beans, drained and rinsed

25 g (1 oz) dark, bitter chocolate (Mexican if possible), grated

1 firm, ripe avocado

¹/2 red onion, chopped

250 g (9 oz/1 cup) sour cream

SERVES 6

Trim the beef of excess fat and cut into cubes. Put the beef, tomatoes, capsicum, mushrooms, onion, garlic, chilli, cumin, cinnamon, sugar and bay leaves in the slow cooker. Pour the stock over the beef and vegetables and cook on low for 6 hours, or until the beef is tender.

Stir in half the coriander, the kidney beans and chocolate. Season with salt and extra chopped chilli if desired. Cook for a further 5 minutes, or until the beans are warmed through.

Chop the avocado and mix with the red onion and remaining coriander leaves. Top each serving of chilli beef with a spoonful of sour cream and a spoonful of the avocado mixture.

PREPARATION TIME: 30 MINUTES   COOKING TIME: 6 HOURS

TURKISH MEATBALLS
WITH RICE

used ground turkey (~2 lbs)

500 g (1 lb 2 oz) minced (ground) beef

$^1/_2$ teaspoon allspice

1 teaspoon ground cinnamon

2 teaspoons ground cumin

1 teaspoon ground coriander

330 g (11$^1/_2$ oz/1$^1/_2$ cups) par-cooked
short-grain rice

375 ml (13 fl oz/1$^1/_2$ cups) chicken stock

400 g (14 oz) tinned chopped tomatoes

35 g (1$^1/_4$ oz/$^1/_4$ cup) toasted
pistachio nuts

2 tablespoons currants

2 tablespoons chopped coriander
(cilantro) leaves

Added 2 small onions, chopped.

SERVES 4–6

Put the beef in a bowl and add the allspice, $^1/_2$ teaspoon of the
cinnamon, 1 teaspoon of the cumin and $^1/_2$ teaspoon of the coriander.
Season with salt and freshly ground black pepper. Using your hands, mix
the spices and beef together well. Roll the mixture into small balls.

Put the meatballs in the slow cooker along with the remaining spices, the
rice, stock and tomatoes. Cook on high for 4 hours, or until the meatballs
and rice are cooked through. Stir through the pistachios, currants and
coriander before serving.

PREPARATION TIME: 30 MINUTES   COOKING TIME: 4 HOURS

ROSEMARY INFUSED LAMB
AND LENTIL CASSEROLE

1 kg (2 lb 4 oz) boned lamb leg

1 onion, thinly sliced

2 garlic cloves, crushed

1 small carrot, finely chopped

2 teaspoons finely chopped fresh ginger

2 teaspoons rosemary leaves

500 ml (17 fl oz/2 cups) lamb or
chicken stock

185 g (6$^1/_2$ oz/1 cup) green or brown lentils

1 tablespoon soft brown sugar

2 teaspoons balsamic vinegar

rosemary sprigs, to garnish

SERVES 6

Trim the lamb of excess fat and cut into 4 cm (1$^1/_2$ inch) cubes. Put the
lamb, onion, garlic, carrot, ginger, rosemary, stock and lentils in the slow
cooker. Cook on high for 4 hours.

Stir through the brown sugar and vinegar and cook for a further 1 hour, or
until the lentils are cooked and the lamb is tender. Season to taste with
salt and freshly ground black pepper, and garnish with rosemary sprigs.

PREPARATION TIME: 20 MINUTES   COOKING TIME: 5 HOURS

HARIRA

500 g (1 lb 2 oz) boneless lamb shoulder
steaks
1 onion, chopped
2 garlic cloves, crushed
1^1/$_2$ teaspoons ground cumin
2 teaspoons paprika
^{1}/$_2$ teaspoon ground cloves
1 bay leaf
750 ml (26 fl oz/3 cups) chicken stock
500 g (1 lb 2 oz/2 cups) tomato passata
(puréed tomatoes)
600 g (1 lb 5 oz) tinned chickpeas,
drained and rinsed
200 g (7 oz/1 cup) par-cooked
long-grain rice
2 large handfuls coriander (cilantro)
leaves, chopped

SERVES 6

Trim the lamb of excess fat and cut into bite-sized cubes. Combine the lamb, onion, garlic, cumin, paprika, cloves, bay leaf, stock, 500 ml (17 fl oz/2 cups) water and the tomato passata in the slow cooker. Cook on low for 5 hours, or until the lamb is tender.

Add the chickpeas and rice and cook for a further 30 minutes, or until the rice is tender. Stir through the coriander and serve.

PREPARATION TIME: 25 MINUTES   COOKING TIME: 5^1/$_2$ HOURS

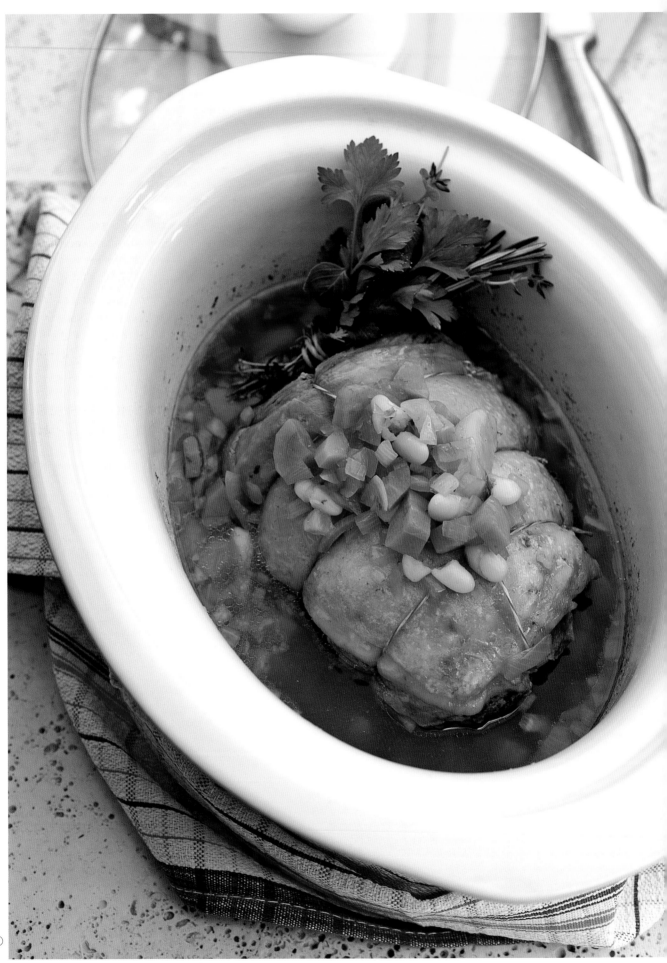

LAMB WITH WHITE BEANS

1 kg (2 lb 4 oz) boned lamb shoulder
2 carrots, diced
2 large onions, chopped
2 garlic cloves, unpeeled
1 bouquet garni
125 ml (4 fl oz/^{1}/$_2$ cup) dry red wine
125 ml (4 fl oz/^{1}/$_2$ cup) chicken stock
400 g (14 oz) tinned cannellini beans,
drained and rinsed

SERVES 4

Tie the lamb with kitchen string to keep its shape. Rub the lamb all over with salt and freshly ground black pepper.

Put the lamb, carrot, onion, garlic, bouquet garni, wine and stock in the slow cooker. Cook on high for 4 hours, or until the lamb is tender.

Lift the lamb out of the slow cooker, cover and leave to rest for 10 minutes. Discard the bouquet garni. Skim the excess fat from the surface of the liquid in the slow cooker, then add the beans. Cook, uncovered, for a further 10–15 minutes, or until the beans are heated through and the sauce has thickened slightly. Season to taste with salt and freshly ground black pepper.

Carve the lamb and arrange on a platter. Spoon the beans around the lamb and drizzle with the sauce. Serve the remaining sauce separately.

PREPARATION TIME: 15 MINUTES   COOKING TIME: 4^1/$_4$ HOURS

SPICED LAMB WITH RED LENTILS

SPICE MIX
2 teaspoons ground cumin
1 teaspoon ground coriander
$1/2$ teaspoon ground turmeric
pinch chilli flakes

750 g (1 lb 10 oz) boneless lamb leg
or shoulder
1 large onion, diced
1 carrot, diced
2 celery stalks, including a few leaves,
diced
125 g ($4^1/2$ oz) green beans, trimmed and
cut into 4 cm ($1^1/2$ inch) lengths
1 tablespoon grated fresh ginger
2 garlic cloves, chopped
500 ml (17 fl oz/2 cups) beef stock
or water
250 g (9 oz/1 cup) tomato passata
(puréed tomatoes) or tomato
pasta sauce
1 tablespoon lemon juice
200 g (7 oz/1 cup) red lentils
1 small handful coriander (cilantro) leaves

SERVES 4

To make the spice mix, combine the ground cumin, coriander, turmeric and chilli flakes in a large bowl.

Trim the lamb of excess fat and cut into 2 cm ($3/4$ inch) cubes. Add the lamb to the spice mix and toss well to thoroughly coat in the spices. Add the onion, carrot, celery and celery leaves, beans, ginger and garlic and stir to combine.

Transfer the lamb and vegetables to the slow cooker and stir in the stock, tomato passata, lemon juice and lentils. Season well with salt and freshly ground black pepper. Cook on high for 4–6 hours, or until the lamb is very tender and the lentils are cooked. The mixture will become thicker the longer it is cooked, so add a little extra stock or water if necessary. Taste and season again with salt and freshly ground black pepper.

To serve, pile onto plates and garnish with coriander leaves. Serve with basmati rice or warmed flat bread.

PREPARATION TIME: 30 MINUTES   COOKING TIME: 4–6 HOURS

LAMB SHANKS WITH BARLEY AND ROOT VEGETABLES

165 g (5³/4 oz/³/4 cup) pearl barley
1 onion, chopped
3 garlic cloves, crushed
1 large carrot, cut into 4 cm (1¹/2 inch) pieces
1 large parsnip, cut into 4 cm (1¹/2 inch) pieces
1 swede (rutabaga) or turnip, cut into 4 cm (1¹/2 inch) pieces
4 Frenched lamb shanks (about 1.2 kg/ 2 lb 10 oz), trimmed of all fat (see Note)
1 teaspoon dried oregano
800 g (1 lb 12 oz) tinned chopped tomatoes
2 tablespoons tomato paste (concentrated purée)
125 ml (4 fl oz/¹/2 cup) white wine or water
1 rosemary sprig
small rosemary sprigs, extra, to garnish

SERVES 4

Put the barley in a bowl and add plenty of water to cover. Soak for 8 hours, or overnight, then drain and place in the base of the slow cooker.

Put the onion, garlic, carrot, parsnip and swede on top of the barley. Top with the lamb shanks, arranged in one layer. Sprinkle over the oregano and pour over the combined tomatoes, tomato paste and wine. Tuck in the rosemary sprig. Season well with salt and freshly ground black pepper.

Cook on low for 8–10 hours, or until the lamb and barley are tender. Remove the rosemary. Skim off any surface fat.

To serve, remove the lamb shanks to a side plate. Spoon the barley and vegetable mixture into wide serving bowls, top each with a shank and garnish with a small rosemary sprig.

PREPARATION TIME: 30 MINUTES +   COOKING TIME: 8–10 HOURS

NOTE: You need to use Frenched lamb shanks so they fit snugly into the slow cooker in one layer.

PERSIAN LAMB WITH CHICKPEAS

750 g (1 lb 10 oz) boneless lamb leg
or shoulder
1 teaspoon ground cinnamon
1 teaspoon allspice
1 teaspoon freshly grated nutmeg
1 large onion, chopped
2 garlic cloves, chopped
200 g (7 oz) eggplant (aubergine), cut into
2 cm (³/4 inch) dice
1 carrot, chopped
1 zucchini (courgette), chopped
400 g (14 oz) tinned chopped tomatoes
60 ml (2 fl oz/¹/4 cup) lemon juice
1 tablespoon tomato paste
(concentrated purée)
400 g (14 oz) tinned chickpeas, drained
and rinsed
90 g (3¹/4 oz/³/4 cup) raisins
60 g (2¹/4 oz/¹/2 cup) slivered almonds,
toasted
1 small handful mint, to garnish

SERVES 4–6

Trim the lamb of excess fat and cut into 2 cm (³/4 inch) cubes. Put the lamb in the slow cooker, sprinkle over the cinnamon, allspice and nutmeg and season with 1 teaspoon salt and some freshly ground black pepper. Stir to combine. Stir in the onion, garlic, eggplant, carrot and zucchini.

Pour in the tomatoes and lemon juice and add the tomato paste. Add the chickpeas and raisins and stir well. Cook for 4–6 hours, or until the lamb is very tender.

To serve, spoon into serving bowls and scatter over the almonds and mint leaves. Serve with basmati rice and plain yoghurt if desired.

PREPARATION TIME: 30 MINUTES   COOKING TIME: 4–6 HOURS

NOTE: Replace the chickpeas with 400 g (14 oz) tinned red kidney beans if preferred.

LAMB BIRYANI

1 kg (2 lb 4 oz) boneless lamb leg
or shoulder
8 cm (3¼ inch) piece fresh ginger,
grated
2 garlic cloves, crushed
2 tablespoons garam masala
½ teaspoon chilli powder
½ teaspoon ground turmeric
2 green chillies, finely chopped
250 g (9 oz/1 cup) Greek-style yoghurt
2 onions, thinly sliced
½ teaspoon saffron threads
2 tablespoons hot milk
400 g (14 oz/2 cups) par-cooked
basmati rice
40 g (1½ oz) butter
1 handful coriander (cilantro) leaves,
chopped (optional)

SERVES 6

Trim the lamb of excess fat and cut into 3 cm (1 inch) cubes. Put the lamb in a bowl with the ginger, garlic, garam masala, chilli powder, turmeric, chilli and yoghurt. Combine well to coat the lamb in the marinade. Cover and marinate in the refrigerator overnight.

Put the lamb and marinade in the slow cooker along with the onion and ¼ teaspoon salt. Cook on low for 6 hours, or until the lamb is tender.

Put the saffron in a bowl with the hot milk and set aside for 10 minutes to soak.

Spread the rice evenly over the lamb in the slow cooker. Dot the rice with the butter and drizzle with the saffron and milk. Cook for a further 1 hour, or until the rice is tender. Garnish with coriander if desired and serve immediately.

PREPARATION TIME: 25 MINUTES +   COOKING TIME: 7 HOURS

INDEX

INDEX